John Baker Hopkins

Cosmopolitan Sketches

John Baker Hopkins

Cosmopolitan Sketches

ISBN/EAN: 9783743351240

Manufactured in Europe, USA, Canada, Australia, Japa

Cover: Foto ©ninafisch / pixelio.de

Manufactured and distributed by brebook publishing software (www.brebook.com)

John Baker Hopkins

Cosmopolitan Sketches

COSMOPOLITAN SKETCHES.

BY

JOHN BAKER HOPKINS.

LONDON:—H. HOLLOWAY, 291, STRAND.
NEW YORK:—WILLMER & ROGERS.
AND AT THE RAILWAY BOOK STALLS.
1867.

CONTENTS.

	PAGE
Saturday Night Marketing	1
Bubble Blowing	12
The Railway Station	23
A Christmas Vision	32
A Breeding Establishment	42
Two Midnight Meetings	52
In a London Police Court	62
Life in Barracks	68
A Beggars' Supper and a Thieves' Hop	75
Found Dead	84
Constable's Hotel	93
"Mary Anne," A 1 for ever	102
Easter Monday	110
Our Domestic Servants	117
Our Suburban Hotel	127

COSMOPOLITAN SKETCHES.

SATURDAY NIGHT MARKETING.

Mr. and Mrs. Gubbins, with their olive branches, four in number and two of a sort—and "a duke cannot have more sorts of kids," as father says — reside on the first floor of No. 1, Deal Court, Brick Lane, Spitalfields. Mr. Gubbins is a carpenter, and Mrs. Gubbins adds to the family revenue by a partnership in the ground-floor-back mangle. The Gubbinses are the great folks and envy of Deal Court, and are considered rather stuck-up people. Thanks to hard work and frugality they are pretty well to do. They have a banking account at the Post-office; Gubbins belongs to a sick and burial society; and his provident wife, about the middle of June, joins two Christmas clubs—one at the "public," from which she gets a fat goose and a bottle of gin; and the other at the grocer's, from which she derives a new shilling, and plums and peel enough to compound a pudding which makes one dyspeptic to think upon. Mrs. Gubbins is brown, squabby, and on the eternity side of forty. Mr. Gubbins is about the same age, and looks as healthy as a man can do who works for ten hours a day, fares moderately, and sleeps in an atmosphere terribly overcharged with nitrogen.

It is half-past six on Saturday night. A tub of grimy suds is before the fire. The last Gubbins offshoot, *ætat.* five years, is on a truckle bedstead in a corner of the reception-room. Offshoot No. 2 is being rubbed down by the eldest daughter, the fair Jemima. The mother is engaged in the needful weekly performance of scouring the family heir. All the darling children (Jemima excepted) are undergoing their Saturday wash. Hence the tub of water and its griminess. The junior branches being in bed, Mr. Gubbins puts down his pipe, Mrs. Gubbins puts on her bonnet and shawl, and Miss Jemima arrays herself in a hat, from beneath which there hangs a net containing the young lady's hair, which by the tallowy light of the room looks like a collection of alarmed kittens' tails. Father pockets a half-pint medicine bottle, mother and daughter each take a large basket, and thus equipped they sally forth to market. Not, however, before Mrs. Gubbins with maternal solicitude has exhorted the ground-floor-back mangle to go to the children if they cry. The ground-floor-back mangle, who has a vision of something short and strong, in the form of *speerits*, about two hours later, readily promises to look after the brats.

Through November mud and November darkness, the latter rendered uncomfortably visible by London gas, glimmering through dirty and unfrequent lamps, the Gubbinses, discussing to-morrow's dinner, *en route*, walk through sundry by-streets, until they emerge in Shoreditch, and behold a scene not easily described and never to be forgotten.

No darkness now, but light—glaring light! Tradesman vies with tradesman in consuming gas. The unprotected burners at the butchers, the greengrocers, the fishmongers, and the tripe shops, are flaring and flickering, and make a loud rumbling noise as they battle with the wind. On either side of the road there is an uninterrupted mile of stalls lighted with unrefined oils, which emit a smell as much unlike attar of roses as any smell can well be. At these stalls everything useful and decorative is to be bought, save coffins and anchors, and rouge for faded cheeks.

Fish that were alive a week ago, vegetables that have not been in London more than a fortnight, crockery-ware warranted to be China, children's toys cheap and frail —it is really very wicked that the children of the poor should be indulged in any such extravagancies as toys— benevolent eel-pies—that is, pies made with unskinned eels —oysters too large and tough to be swallowed without chewing, apples rather the worse for time at a penny a pound—cutlery that looks in the unrefined light as though it might possibly cut, and haberdashery dirt cheap. The male and female stall-keepers call out their wares without ceasing, and almost drown the voices of the butchers who are hoarsely persuading Her Majesty's subjects to "Buy, buy, buy!" To add to the confusion, there is the wonderful cheap Jack, with a miscellaneous collection in his cart, and who does not mind presenting every customer who will invest a sixpence with a gold ring—"None of your Brummagem stuff, my dears, but 'all-marked." A little way off is the itinerant quack: "Is there anything the matter with you? Have you got the rheumatism, mum? Has your good man got the bile? Have your children got the worms? This candy, at a penny a stick, will cure all complaints. It is made by the Indians, was always used by the Duke of Wellington, and is eaten by the Queen every night before going to bed, by order of the Lord Mayor." At a corner of a street is a nigger band, singing and delighting the listeners. Execrable singing we admit, but, on the whole, not much worse than the drawing-room ballad singing one is sometimes obliged to hear; and, alas! to applaud. On the other side of the way is an opposition—to wit, two men selling flimsy sheets of songs, and shouting title and words as they sell them. They do a thriving trade, and a continuous stream of copper flows into their capacious pockets.

The pavement is crowded. If anyone is in a hurry he must take to the road. Such a seething and incongruous mass of humanity! Decently clad wives of City clerks who have to keep up appearances upon £100 a-year, and who have come a long distance to buy the necessaries of life cheaply. Mechanics' wives comfortably clad, who evidently enjoy the marketing. Women in unwomanly rags. Girls with their sweethearts. Children who were better at home. Those who are homeless and who find that the poor are prone to take compassion on the wretched, frequent shoreditch on Saturday nights. Drunken men and drunken women. Take it altogether, a bewildering scene to the novice.

But the Gubbins family are not in the least disconcerted by the noise and the bustling crowd. They stop before a vendor of whelks, and each has a little white saucer full of a small glutinous fish floating in a greenish oily-looking gravy. In addition to this, Miss Jemima, who is a growing girl of thirteen years, is treated to a hot potatoe, which, with a sprinkling of salt and a small pinch of what passes for butter, cost the modest sum of one halfpenny. Mr. Gubbins, who is a fond parent—you see the working classes have their weaknesses—invests threepence in toys for the bairns at Deal Court. These preliminaries over, the serious business of the evening commences.

First to the butcher's. Such a show of meat, though ribs and sirloins of beef are conspicuous by their absence. When a family has to be kept upon rather less than 30s. a week, it will not do to pay 10d. per pound for bone, to be resold at $\frac{1}{2}$d. per pound. So the best cuts go westward. Mrs. Gubbins is a meat critic. The butcher shows her a piece of beef. She plunges her fingers into it, and shakes her head. She does not like the feel of it, it is too flabby. Will she take the knuckle end of a leg of mutton? No, it cuts to nothing. Her eye lights upon a piece of pork. She examines the skin. All right, there is no trace of the measles. She looks at the fat. It is hard as lard, and nearly as white. The pork is the thing. It is weighed, and she goes to a little glass box to pay the butcher's wife, whose red and juicy appearance is a proof that the smell of meat is salubrious. At this point there is a slight row between Mrs. Gubbins and her husband. Mrs. Gubbins can tell you in the twinkling of an eye what three dozen and six of mangling come to at 1½d. a dozen, but when the question is 5lb. 2oz. of meat at 8½d. per lb., she is at the mercy of the butcher's wife. She tries to reckon it with her fingers and signally fails. She appeals to Gubbins, but she might as well ask him to calculate the transit of the planet Venus. Gubbins says no doubt the young woman is correct. Mrs. Gubbins says he does not care how she's put upon, thrusts the pork into Jemima's basket, counts her change, and leaves the shop, firmly persuaded that she has been cheated by the butcher, neglected by her husband, and is a very badly-used woman. Yet, Mrs. Gubbins, you excited the envy of the woman who was buying bullock's liver—bullock's liver pudding is cheap and satisfying food—and who wished she could afford to buy pork.

Next door, to the greengrocer's. After trying several cabbages, Mrs. Gubbins selects a big-hearted one; then buys some potatoes—not kidneys, but Yorkshire reds. Gubbins is cheerful, and Jemima's mouth waters. Won't it be jolly to-morrow? The earthenware baking dish, which is divided into two compartments, will be brought into requisition. Into one compartment the potatoes will be sliced and sprinkled over with salt. In the other compartment there will be batter pudding. Over both, on an iron stand, will be the pork. It will go to the baker's just as the genteel world is going to church. As the meat gets warm, fat will rain down upon the pudding and upon the potatoes, and won't they be rich? Mrs. Gubbins, careful wife, has a very deep baking-dish. She will not let the baker have her fat. Not she, indeed. Oh, that pudding, Jemima! Oh, those potatoes, rather pale-looking and soddened, but so uncommonly greasy!

Now for a surprise! Does not Gubbins recollect what to-morrow is? "Lor, I never see such a man as Gubbins. Why, wasn't to-morrow their wedding-day?" Therefore,

Mrs. Gubbins bought some apples, so that, in addition to the rich batter, there would be apple pudding. Jemima was in ecstacies. Gubbins was obliged to calm his feelings by chewing a quid of tobacco. Won't there be a scene tomorrow when mother peels the apples? Won't the children snatch at the peel and devour it with inordinate relish? Won't mother cut out big cores to please her little flock? Fat pork, fat potatoes, fat batter, apple pudding with suet crust. Oh, how supremely vulgar and coarse! Strasbourg pie. The diseased livers of geese. Oh, how supremely genteel! Gubbins, why don't you mend your manners, eschew fat pork, and eat *pate fois de gras?*

Jemima is sent home with meat, potatoes, and apples. She is to go straight home, and not to gossip. Jemima is tolerably obedient, yet before she gets to the parental first floor she will let all the world of Deal Court know about the fat pork and the apple pudding. The Deal Court community is as curious about the Gubbinses' Sunday dinner as the lower middle classes are to know whether the Queen walked in the Park or on the Slopes.

Jemima being despatched home, Mr. and Mrs. Gubbins enter one of the numerous palaces—gin palaces—of Shoreditch. They go into what is called the private bar, at which pipe-smoking is forbidden, and "heavy wet," that is porter, is not served. Mr. Gubbins brings out his half-pint medicine bottle, and requests the youth behind the bar to fill it with "Old Tom," and to give him a pint of the beery mixture known as "Cooper." The barman having drawn the beer and blown into the pewter to see if it was full, and Mr. Gubbins having blown away the froth, hands the flowing tankard to his wife. Gubbins is anxious. His better-half is rather partial to beer, and generally leaves him the worser half-pint. Saturday is such a busy day with Mrs. Gubbins. There is helping to get home the mangling; there is cleaning the place; there is cleaning the children, which Mrs. Gubbins says is equal to standing for six hours at the wash-tub. If, then, she drinks more than her share, she is to be forgiven. Mr. and Mrs. Gubbins having refreshed, visit the grocer's, where amongst other things, Mrs. Gubbins will buy a quarter of a pound of tea. Well, to be sure, it is a crush to get into the grocer's. Gubbins does not attempt it, but leaves his wife to fight it out, and meantime goes to the tobacconist's for his usual supply of the weed. Sly Mr. Gubbins! Does not a fascinating damsel vend the tobacco? Clever young woman! All her male customers are enraptured with her, but the female snuff-takers consider her "a 'orrid and hodious cat." Gubbins is as innocent as a lamb, yet enjoys the unfounded idea that the young damsel is a little taken with him.

At length Mrs. Gubbins is nearing the grocer's counter What a splendid text for an anthem of praise does that shop afford! Do you deny that a cup of tea is a boon? Years ago the poorer classes could not afford to drink good tea, but they can do so now. Not by reason of free trade only, but through a countless number of agencies. To buy that quarter of a pound of tea with the limited means of Mrs. Gubbins the labours of the Free-traders were indeed necessary, but not these only. Those who advanced and improved the art of navigation, those whose valour and diplomacy opened China and India to the commerce of the world— those who invented machinery by which England is enabled to clothe the East—all these and ten thousand other noble and wise deeds were necessary preliminaries to Mrs. Gubbins getting a quarter of a pound of mixed tea for $8\frac{1}{2}$d. How the Ruler of all the Earth has circumscribed the influence of our selfishness! We may labour for fame, or for riches, or for family, or for a class, but whatsoever good thing we do is done unto all mankind. It may or may not be that this principle is equally true of evil, but it is certain that whatever good we do is not interred with our bones, but is an everlasting and, so far as mankind is concerned, a universal benefit. Mrs. Gubbins, of course, does not bother herself with philosophy. To her the tea only suggests the thought of a warm drink. Being served, she rejoins Gubbins, who is slightly pensive and, perhaps, penitent in respect to the tobacco-shop enchantress.

Soon after nine our couple return to Deal Court. The children are safe and sleeping. At least, they are pretending to sleep, for Jemima has been entertaining them with an account of the marketing, and the arrangements for the Sunday dinner. So much, then, for the Saturday night marketing of the Gubbinses! Putting aside the little disagreeables, the lack of refinement, and the time of night, it is, after all, not an unpleasant picture to look upon. Would to God such was the invariable character of Saturday night marketing in London!

Once more to Shoreditch. Do you see that woman stealing out of the pawnbroker's—tall, thin, haggard, and dressed in draggling black? She has just received a few shillings on a pair of blankets and on some child's clothing—only fourpence on the latter, and she let fall a tear when she parted with the little bundle. See her glide into the baker's for some bread, and into the chandler's for some candles, and then home. Let us follow her. In the worst room of perhaps the worst house of Spitalfields, see her sitting. Where is her husband? Oh! dead, months ago. Her eldest daughter, the same age as Jemima Gubbins, is away doing a little charing for a tradesman at twopence per day and her board. Her boy has been apprenticed by the parish. She has a third child in the room with her—a fair-haired child, the pet of the family. It was five years old yesterday. It is in bed. It was this child's clothes the mother pawned—oh, how cruel! No matter! the child is dead, and will never need them more. "What a relief to the wretched mother!" says the parish poor law guardian. Ah, wretched mother, indeed! To bury her child will cost her about three shillings more than she has been able to get together. She goes to the bed—well, well, to the straw—on which her child is lying. Death in this case was as much like sleep as it can be, yet even then it was fearfully different. The mother cried, never thinking that it was a relief to lose her child. These poor people are not political economists. It was noteworthy how, as she turned from the bed, she tucked in the tattered cloak that covered her child, as though the little one was only dozing, and might get cold. She knew it was dead; but a mother does not easily realise that her child is but clay—but clay. The outburst of grief is over, the candle is lighted, and she begins to sew. Let her persevere—and if her taskmaster is not worse than the average—she may earn nearly a penny an hour. The door opens. The daughter has returned from her day's work. She kisses her mother affectionately, and the mother caresses her child. And the mother is touched with the sorrow of her girl; and, to lighten it, tries for a moment to forget her heavy bereavement. She endeavours to look cheerful, and almost succeeds, and reproaches her child with giving way to grief. The girl has looked towards the bed, and is sobbing.

"Mother," says the girl, "let us go and buy the coffin."

"On Monday," says the mother, pointing to the work on the table.

"We've got it, mother; missus heard of our loss, and gave me that," said the girl, putting down five shillings on the table.

Then the mother went to the little bed, and her girl was by her side, and they kissed the child, and with a piece of tape measured it. Then they went to the Saturday night market. First to the pawnbrokers, and redeemed the little bundle of the dead child's clothing. "We will keep them now," said the widow. Then to the undertaker's. It was a large and thriving establishment. The shop was filled with coffins of all sizes, and men were busy nailing the cloth on a coffin that had to be sent home that night. The widow paid the undertaker the stipulated price, and he told her that the funeral could take place on the morrow. Undertakers do not give credit to poor people. He promised that the child should be buried like a lady. Well, he was not so very wrong. Even an undertaker cannot cheat the dead. Dust to dust, ashes to ashes, happens to all, no matter how pompous or how plain the funeral. Plumes and trappings do not inspire, nor does their absence deprive us of the hope of immortality. It comforted the widow and her daughter to be told that the child would be buried like a lady. There was no sin in that feeling of pride.

The widow produced the piece of tape, the measure of the dead child, and the undertaker gave her a plain deal coffin, As the widow's scanty shawl would not cover it, he wrapped it for her in a piece of sacking—the sacking to be returned. The mother and daughter hasten home with their marketing. At the door the son is waiting—afraid, poor boy, to go alone into the chamber of death. They enter the room, and the candle is lighted. The mother places the coffin on the table, and goes to the truckle bedstead. The frighted boy clings to his sister, and the widow sobs and moans in the bitterness of her affliction.

"Oh! what shall we do, what shall we do now?" exclaimed the girl.

The mother heard the cry, and remembered the living. She could not speak, but she came to her children and kissed them. Then she took the coffin, and, with the girl holding the candle, again went to the truckle bedstead. The boy tried to follow them, but he could not. He sat on the chair, and covered his face in his mother's work.

The widow set down the coffin, and the candle was placed near to it. She saw that her girl was very pale, and she smiled upon her to encourage her. And the girl kissed her mother. Then the mother and the girl lifted the dead child as gently as if they feared to wake her, and laid her in the coffin. The death coldness struck their hearts, and they trembled a little. And the mother cut off three locks of hair—one for each of the living. Then she went to her boy, and cut off some of his hair, then of her girl's, then of her own, and she put the hair upon the bosom of the dead. And she brought the boy, half dragging him to the coffin, and the brother and the mother and the sister kissed the dead child.

By an instinct they knelt down. They used no form of prayer. Grief had stricken them dumb. But our Father in heaven hears the unspoken prayer of affliction.

To bed, then, just as the chimes from a hundred church clocks are proclaiming the hour of midnight and the advent of Sunday. To bed—mother, daughter, and son—huddling close to each other. To bed, and it may be to sleep. It may be to dream—and in the dream to recall the teachings of the Sunday-school, and to see the dead child no longer dead. To see her in the ineffable light and glory of the Celestial City, clothed in white robes, crowned with an immortal crown, and with ten thousand thousand angels singing songs of praise. Nay, even hearing in the dream the everlasting anthem.

Thank God it is not all a dream. A few hours later, when the widow and her children stand by the open grave, and the earth rattles on the deal coffin, the priest will tell them that the grave has not gotten the victory, and that the dead child shall on *that* day rise again. And the terror of the children will from day to day decrease, and the widow will not mourn as one without hope.

BUBBLE-BLOWING.

THE antecedents of Mr. Thaddeus Flyer are a mystery to his acquaintance. Who were his parents, what they were, and where they lived, are among the things not generally known. Mr. Flyer is rich, but how he became rich is a secret that baffles the curiosity of his neighbours. It is, however, enough for society that Mr. Flyer exists, that he is a highly-respected gentleman, that he has a very proper establishment, that his dinners are excellent, and that his wines delight the palate and exhilarate the spirits, without involving the penalties of soda-water and headache in the morning.

Mr. Thaddeus Flyer and all his belongings inspire an idea of most solid respectability. The worthy gentleman is a portly individual, verging on fifty. His features are a cross between Saxon nobility and Amsterdam Judaism. His iron grey hair is cropped short, his lip and chin are thoroughly effeminated by the razor, his whiskers are so precisely arranged that a magnifying glass would not disclose a single hair awry; his feet are small, his hands are ditto, and very white; his dress is generally black, and the only indications of jewellery are a signet ring, a very valuable diamond ring, and half-a-dozen links of a massive gold chain. Mr. Flyer resides in a square near to Regent Street, in an old-fashioned substantial mansion. The furniture and appointments are in unexceptionable taste. Whilst they testify to the pecuniary resources of the host, there is no vulgar show or pretension. The carpets are of subdued colours, but so thick that the creekiest of boots pass over them in silence. The walls are covered with costly pictures in neat frames. The plate is heavy, but old-fashioned. Neither the somewhat stout butler, nor the tall servant-boy is in livery. From first to last Mr. Flyer and his establishment are the types of unspeculative and Three-per-Cent. Consols respectability.

Mr. Flyer is a bachelor, and quite a pet with the majority of the double f.—fair and frail—sex, as he, to his batchelor friends, facetiously describes the sweeter half of mankind. Mothers with marriageable daughters hate him as in duty bound. What can be a more pernicious example to young men than a happy and well-to-do bachelor of fifty? In their maternal solicitude these dames invent and circulate naughty calumnies about Mr. Flyer; but for all that he is a prodigious favourite with widows and with forlorn maidens who are forced to resort to rouge, to pearl powder, to false locks, and false teeth, to mask the evidences of advancing years. When Mr. Flyer is chaffed about his single blessedness by married men, he says:—"I love and respect the sex. I do not want to be cured of this amiable and pleasant weakness, and therefore I do not marry." But, though a bachelor, Mr. Flyer leads an unexceptionably regular life. He has a family pew at the parish church, and every Sunday morning he may be seen at two minutes to eleven gracefully leaning on the pew-door worshipping the inside of the crown of his hat. He subscribes munificently to local charities, but he does not allow his name to be published. His humility does not go unrewarded, for his unostentatious benevolence is the theme of conversation in his circle. Mr. Flyer is *proper—not pious. With him religion is only a social duty, and he goes to church because it is etiquette for the head of a respectable establishment to do so. He is fond of hunting and shooting, though he does not keep a country establishment. He says he finds London is the best hunting county, for by the railways he can go to half-a-dozen of the finest meets, and be home in time for a quiet dinner. He plays at billiards moderately well, but never wins much. He plays at whist very well, but will not exceed crown points. He objects to gambling on principle. He is a very abstemious man. His guests may drink what they please; but he never imbibes more than two glasses of sherry mixed with water. He keeps first-rate cigars for his visitors, but he does not smoke. Mr. Flyer is free from small failings. He is neither slow nor fast; he hits the credit medium of perfect respectability.

But Mr. Flyer is not an idle man. In his well-appointed mansion is a study, and in this study Mr. Flyer works many hours per day. He is not an author or a politician. He devotes his genius and time to the furtherance of the trading interests of England. In a word, he is a promoter of joint-stock enterprise. He is a Bubble-Blower. Perhaps five per cent. of the new undertakings that are announced in London are due to his activity. Yet his connection with them is never avowed. Why should so bright a light be hidden under a bushel? We shall be doing a service to our generation, and be giving Mr. Flyer his deserts by rescuing his name from oblivion, and setting forth how he assists in the development of the material resources of the country. We propose to do so by describing how he blew the bubble of Smith, Jones, and Co. (Limited).

Messrs. Smith, Jones, and Co. are a firm who have a counting-house in a little place in Gracechurch Street. Mr. Smith had been unfortunate in bygone years, and had on more than one occasion been compelled to seek that protection which the laws of the land give to insolvent debtors against their importunate creditors. Mr. Jones had been connected with the coal trade on commission. The Co. was a myth. The worthy Mr. Smith and the not less worthy Mr. Jones, upon a capital of a very limited amount, entered into the wine trade. Not to put too fine a point upon it, we may state that the capital of Messrs. Smith and Jones was what may be called algebraically a minus quantity. They began without property and with debts. Being ingenious and persevering, they succeeded in getting goods on long credit and selling them for cash. There is a popular notion that if a trader sells his goods for less than he pays for them he cannot live. This is a fallacy. Smith, Jones, and Co. dressed well, lived well, and kept up charming suburban establishments; yet, as a rule, their wines cost them 25 per cent. more than they realised. Amongst their customers was Mr. Thaddeus Flyer. It happened that the Joint Stock Bank favoured with the account of Smith, Jones, and Co., from some unaccountable reason, informed the firm that they could discount no more bills at present. This was awkward, as Smith, Jones, and Co. did not stand well in the open Market. One bill-broker to whom they applied for accommodation had the impudence to intimate that he would rather discount brown paper without any signatures at all, for then he might use it for packing parcels, but that the bills of Smith, Jones, and Co. were useless as well as valueless. In this fix, Mr. Smith, the senior partner, called upon Mr. Thaddeus Flyer, to see if that gentleman was inclined to assist the firm in its difficulties. Mr. Flyer at once perceived that there was a favourable opportunity for the exercise of his patriotic benevolence. He told Mr. Smith that his difficulties arose from the want of sufficient capital, to which proposition Mr. Smith fully assented. The disease was indisputable, what was the remedy? Mr. Flyer suggested the formation of a joint-stock company, limited; and Mr. Smith was delighted with the suggestion.

The books of the firm were placed in the hands of a clever accountant, who from them concocted a balance-sheet of a most satisfactory aspect. It appeared, though neither Mr. Smith nor Mr. Jones knew it, that the profits of the firm were many thousands a-year. Smith, Jones, and Co. were shippers. For example: they bought sham Champagne in Germany at 16s. per dozen. This they sent to India and the colonies invoiced at 60s. per dozen, receiving an advance from London houses at the rate of 25s. per dozen. It was the same with other wines. As the firm had not been very long establised, no account sales had been received from India or the colonies, and the wines were set down in the books and on the balance sheet at the invoice prices. Hence, according to the books the profits were large.

We may here observe that when the wines were sold they did not fetch enough to pay the shipping and other charges. Of course Mr. Smith and Mr. Jones could not be blamed for this result. They are not responsible for the Anglo-Indians and the dons of Australia not relishing Rhine wine converted into Champagne by sugar and gas.

Mr. Flyer was satisfied with the balance-sheet, and forthwith set to work to get up a company. Through an advertisement he engaged a young gentleman as secretary at £500 a-year, who amongst other qualifications had £500 to advance for preliminary expenses. When we say that Mr. Flyer engaged the young gentleman, we mean that he put Mr. Smith in the way of doing so, for Mr. Flyer never interfered in such details. The secretary was congratulated on his good luck in being selected out of nearly two hundred candidates. Mr. Flyer then drew up a prospectus, of which the following is a copy :—

"SMITH, JONES AND CO.

(LIMITED).

CAPITAL, £250,000,

In 50,000 *Shares of* £5 *Each.*

In introducing this important undertaking to the public, the directors feel that a very brief explanation will be sufficient. A glance at the Board of Trade returns for any quarter will show that the wine trade of this opulent country has increased and is increasing. It is for the most part in private hands, yet it offers a legitimate and highly lucrative opportunity for the application of the great joint-stock principle. Much might be written about the enormous social benefits that will accrue from a company that fosters the sale of that which maketh glad the heart of man. Much might be written on the patriotic character of this enterprise, seeing that wine pays a duty, and that the consumption of wine stimulates the foreign commerce of our native land, and so carries to distant seas that glorious flag which has for a thousand years defied the battle and the breeze. These reflections will naturally occur to the Christian and the patriot, and it will recommend 'Smith, Jones, and Co. (Limited)' to their prayers and sympathies. But the duties of the directors are exclusively commercial. The question they have to deal with is this:—Will the company pay? Upon this point it will be enough to state that the business of the wine merchant is only limited by the amount of his capital, and that the average gross profits are not less than 50 per cent.

The directors have purchased, on terms most favourable to the company, the flourishing business of Messrs. Smith, Jones, and Co. The books of the firm have been examined by an eminent accountant, and he reports that the profits of the past six months were over £7,000, or at the rate of £15,000 per annum. For the stock and goodwill, Messrs. Smith, Jones, and Co. have accepted the inadequate sum of £50,000, of which one-third is to be paid in cash, and the other two-thirds in paid-up shares. The shares are not to be parted with until a dividend of 20 per cent. has been declared. Messrs. Smith, Jones, and Co. guarantee a minimum dividend of 10 per cent. for the first two years.

The directors, after careful inquiry, are persuaded that the average dividends will not be less than from 30 to 40 per cent., and that a sounder and more splendid investment is not in the market. The company starts with an established business, and therefore, from the first, there will be an accumulation of profits. The senior partners, Mr. Adolphus Smith and Mr. Jabez Jones, have joined the direction, and, consequently, the company will have the invaluable advantage of their experience.

The directors beg to say that no promotion money will be paid, as they consider that an illegitimate tax upon joint-stock enterprise."

Having prepared the prospectus, Mr. Flyer called on his friend Colonel Rigge, C.B., and proposed to him to become chairman of the company. The Colonel, whose tastes were considerably in advance of his means, was just the man for the post. He only stipulated that he should have no bother, and receive £250 per annum.

"I don't much like going into a trading concern, Flyer."

"Oh, my dear Colonel," said Mr. Flyer, "any other

trade would be detestable, but the wine trade is, in my opinion, the link between commerce and non-trading respectability."

"Shall I have to take any shares, Flyer?"

"Yes, Colonel, but they will cost you nothing. In this company the directors are not presented with their qualifications, for shareholders do not like the system, but they take the required number of shares, and the secretary manages the payment by a sort of legal fiction."

"It seems a good thing, Flyer, why do you not take it yourself?"

"My dear fellow, I have not a handle or a tail to my name. I am neither a Colonel nor a C.B."

"Ah, there is some use in that C.B. after all."

The Colonel was right. He had been living on the strength of it for ten years.

Having secured the chairman, Mr. Flyer was enabled to complete the *dramatis personæ* of the company by correspondence, as he always kept by him a list of men who were ready to go on any board. The direction stood as follows:—

"Colonel Rigge, C.B. (Chairman), Bengalee Club, Pall Mall, and the Rookery, Yorkshire.
Adolphus Smith, Esq., The Cedars, Hampstead.
Jabez Jones, Esq., The Poplars, Putney.
John Sloper, Esq. (late of the firm of Dunn, Sloper, and Co., of Bombay).
George Sprouts, Esq. (late of the firm of Sprouts, Sprouts, and Co., Melbourne).

With power to add to their number.

Bankers.—The Poultry Bank (Limited).
Auditors.—Messrs. Levy, Docket, and Co. (accountants).
Solicitor.—Alfred Faker, Esq.
Brokers.—Messrs. Hornby and Welsher.
Secretary.—Peter Gosling, Esq."

Offices were taken, and elegantly furnished, with Mr.

Gosling's money. The company was advertised upon credit, by an agent, and advertised very extensively. In a few days Mr. Smith called upon Mr. Flyer with rather a long face.

"My dear sir, I see by the papers that the list is to be closed on Saturday, and really we have no applications for shares!"

Mr. Flyer smiled one of his beautiful benevolent smiles.

"Pray make yourself quite easy, my dear Mr. Smith. I am very glad we have few applications. You will see why in the course of a month or so."

The share list is closed, and the directors meet. They appoint an allotment committee, which consists of Colonel Rigge, C.B., Mr. Sloper, and Mr. Sprouts. As the Colonel has gone to Baden-Baden (by the advice of his lawyer) for the benefit of his health, the labour of allotment devolves entirely upon Messrs. Sloper and Sprouts, who act upon the advice (gratis) of Mr. Flyer. About 1,000 shares had been applied for by the public, and these are allotted in full. The number of shares necessary to complete the legal establishment of the company are allotted to the friends of the committee, and are left in the care of the committee.

Then begins the process commonly known as "rigging the market." Some of Mr. Flyer's friends, on his recommendation, are willing to sell, and some are willing to buy, shares at 2 per cent. premium. Forthwith the papers quote the shares at 2 per cent. premium. Those who have had letters of allotment are delighted, and all the prudent ones sell, and sell without any difficulty. Higher and higher goes the price. Some of Mr. Flyer's friends are willing to buy at 4 per cent. premium, and some are willing to sell at 4 per cent. premium, and the consequence is that the shares are quoted at 4 per cent. premium. Mr. Smith now perceives why it would have been inconvenient if there had been too many applications from the public. As it is no one can say that the directors are *macing* the public, for no one can say that his application for shares was refused. The business progresses. The public swallow the bait, and buy at a premium. At length, Mr. Flyer is enabled to get rid of 5,000 shares, at from 4 to 6 per cent. premium. It must not be supposed that Mr. Flyer has made from £10,000 to £20,000 profit. Nothing of the sort. "Rigging the market" is a costly process. So many have to share the spoil, and the market is not inflated without a heavy expenditure. Mr. Flyer, who adopts the system of quick returns, is contented to net about £2,000 by the sale of his shares, and as he knows the exact time when the bubble will burst, he pockets another £1,000 by selling some shares for the account. He does not neglect his friends. He is noted for being liberal with the "swag." Mr. Faker, the solicitor, sells his 200 shares at the right moment. Messrs. Smith and Jones do not make much out of the share transactions—Mr. Flyer would not allow them to have their shares formally allotted—but they get £2,000 of the purchase money out of the first call that is made, and out of that fund the fortunate secretary also gets a quarter's salary.

Have you seen little urchins with soap, water, and clay pipes? It takes some time to get the lather of the proper consistency, and to set a bubble fairly afloat. The collapse is, on the contrary, the work of a moment. So it is with financial bubbles, and so it was with "Smith, Jones, and Co. (Limited)." In less than a year there is an extraordinary meeting of the shareholders. The directors find it their duty to state that their affairs are not so prosperous as they expected, and they place themselves in the hands of their constituents. After a somewhat stormy debate a resolution is passed to wind up the affairs of the company. Mr. Smith and Mr. Jones are regarded as martyrs even by the unfortunate shareholders. These gentlemen, in a most generous spirit, give up their 6,000 paid-up shares, and will look only for the balance of the purchase-money due to them. A winding-up order is obtained. About a hundred shareholders are ruined, including several widows and retired tradesmen, and the creditors, including Messrs. Smith and Jones, get 5s. in the pound.

What can be more admirable than the tact and skill of the benevolent and respectable Mr. Thaddeus Flyer? The money he made cost the company nothing. Messrs. Smith and Jones have learnt that there is an exception to the rule *ex nihilo nihil fit,* for out of less than nothing they have got about £7,000. That the company came to grief is not Mr. Flyer's fault. It is his business to blow bubbles, but not to keep them from bursting. Nor will he be discouraged. He will still devote his inestimable talents to the promotion of joint-stock enterprise, and to the development of the unlimited resources of this great, glorious, free, and Christian country.

Nor will the public be discouraged. No matter what ill-natured persons say, little capitalists will confide in the glowing promises of the adroit bubble-blower. We withdraw that word "adroit." There is no adroitness required to catch gulls who perch upon one's hands and ask to have salt put upon their tails. Mr. Thaddeus Flyer is a type of a class, and " Smith, Jones, and Co. (Limited)," is a type of enterprises that are from week to week launched upon the market. So long as the public are confiding, so long will the Flyers continue to practise the lucrative art of bubble-blowing.

Not that we intend utterly to denounce either the dupes or the dupers. We suppose folly and roguery have their uses. A friend of ours was talking to a Millenniumist. "Sir," he said, "do you mean to say that in the Millennium there will be no war, no crime, no intrigue, and no division?" The Millenniumist told him it would be so. "Then," said our friend, "I am glad that I do not live in the Millennium time. What on earth should I do with my sons? One is a soldier, another is a lawyer, another destined for the church, and my youngest is going to walk the hospitals. Bless, me, sir, if we had the Millennium, there would be no careers for younger sons and genteel poverty!" Undoubtedly

Mr. Flyer's bubbles bring grist to the legal mill. We would, however, respectfully hint that so long as bubble-blowing flourishes in England, it is not wise for us to denounce the gaming tables of Hamburg and Baden. We had better gid rid of the beam that is in our own eye before we complain of the mote that is in the eye of our German cousins.

THE RAILWAY STATION.

———o———

THE preliminaries of a railway journey are generally severe trials of temper to infrequent travellers. If one has to start early in the morning, the night's rest is disturbed by a nervous dread of oversleeping oneself. We awaken up half-a-dozen times, strike a light, and wonder that our watch still indicates the very small hours of the morning, and we are just settling down into a comfortable doze, when the domestic thunders at the door, and warns us that it is time to get up. If the train starts later in the day, we are subjected to a species of worry rather worse than unwonted early rising. With a journey before us, it is impossible to attend to the usual avocations, and the hours drag heavily. We have studied "Bradshaw," and we find that the hour of departure is 1 p.m. We think it is 1 p.m., for "Bradshaw" has been so abused that we are doubtful whether we have rightly construed the indispensable guide. We order the cab at least half-an-hour too soon, and we fume and fret exceedingly because cabby is three minutes and two seconds behind the appointed moment. However, we drive fast, and arrive at the station three-quarters of an hour before the train starts. We endeavour to comfort ourselves by reflecting that as "time and trains wait for no man," it is better to be an hour too early than a minute too late. Likely enough, before we are off, we shall have become persuaded that it is best to be neither too early nor too late, but punctual.

A porter bears off our luggage, with an injunction to us to see it labelled when we have our ticket. When can we obtain our ticket? Ten minutes before the train starts. We have nearly an hour to lounge away, and then we are to have a crush, and scuffle for our ticket. Rather provoking this arrangement, and must be horribly exasperating to the hysterical lady who arrives at the station an hour-and-a-half to soon in order to avoid bother and flurry, and to start in comfort.

We proceed to the waiting-room. It is a lofty and well-furnished apartment. The carpet is dusty Turkey, and the chairs and sofas are soft and easy. Did anyone ever feel jolly in a metropolitan waiting-room? It reminds us of the dining-room of the London physician, into which patients are ushered until their turn comes to see the doctor. We have heard of an unhappy shareholder who, to avenge himself for getting no dividends passes half of his waking hours in a waiting-room. By that means he has the consolation of getting something for his money. What direct pecuniary advantage the gentleman derives we confess is beyond our comprehension, seeing that he has to forsake a comfortable home, for which, meantime, he has to pay, to get his pennyworth out of the railway accommodation. Generally, there are but few persons in the waiting-room, and they look upon the last comer as an intruder upon their privacy. Most likely there are two or three children, who amuse themselves by jumping about the chairs and sofas, to the delight of their fond parents, and to the annoyance of the rest of the company. Wise railway travellers always avoid little dogs, young children, and unprotected females under fifty.

We look at our watch. Twenty-five minutes past twelve. Bah, it must be slow! Exit from the waiting-room to the booking-office. We glance at the clock, and learn that, so far from being slow, our watch is a few minutes fast. We have a spell at the time-table appended to the wall, and so while away a few seconds in tracing the course of our journey. We then read over some placards, which inform us of Jones being fined forty shillings for smoking, of Smith being sent to prison for seven days for assaulting one of the company's officers in the discharge of his duty—it is very rarely that a passenger has a chance of assaulting an officer under such circumstances—and of Robinson being mulcted in ten shillings and costs for leaving a train whilst in motion. We speculate as to whether these are real or fictitious cases. Supposing them to be fictitious, we admire the benevolent cunning of railway managers to prevent their passengers doing wrong. Suppose them to be real, we ask ourselves if it is quite fair, after a man has paid his fine or been to prison, to post him for months? We hear now and then of lords and gentlemen being fined for smoking without first paying a small fine to the guard; but who ever saw such cases posted at a railway-station? It is only poor men whose offences are kept before the public eye. Railway managers are genteelly discreet, as well as sternly just.

We pay a visit to the book-stall, and buy some literature for the journey. Thanks to the enterprise of Messrs. W. H. SMITH and SON, who have done as much to circulate literature as all the other circulating libraries put together, we can obtain everything we want in the way of newspapers, periodicals, or books. Leaving the book-stall, we notice the refreshing announcement of "The Refreshment Room." We are not hungry or thirsty, but it would be as well, perhaps, to provide for prospective hunger and thirst. What can we have? Oh, almost anything except civility, attention, or good viands at a reasonable price. We suppose no one ever visited a railway refreshment-room without feeling himself cruelly victimised. The coffee is cold and execrable, and the milk feathered. The tea resembles a mild decoction of senna. The stout is of fair quality, but deficient in quantity, and a hundred per cent. dearer than at any other place in the United Kingdom. The wine is South African, which may suit the negro stomach, but is poison to the Caucasian stomach. The Cognac, sold in small bottles for the accommodation of travellers, is a British compound of burnt sugar, bad sherry, and spirits of wine. The eatables are worthy of the drinkables. The sandwiches are knify and stale. The buns and biscuits would be rejected by the *habitues* of the New Cut. Do not venture on fowl, unless you are prepared to have your teeth filled with stringy gristle for the remainder of the day. The fowls sold at the railway refreshment-room are not slaughtered, but humanely permitted to die of sheer old age. The young ladies behind the counter are unpleasantly curt in their manner. They attend to you just when it suits them, and they hand you the things as if they were poor-law officers dispensing public alms to casual paupers. Sour damsels, we will not be hard upon you. It must be a wearying occupation to be constantly dispensing bad and dear food to strange and scowling customers. We trust that the poor creatures are not compelled to feed on the stock-in-trade. No, that inhumanity is impossible. Railway refreshment-room fare for six consecutive days would be fatal to the strongest constitution.

It will soon be time to get our ticket, and, meanwhile, we cannot do better than glance at the big world in miniature, the people on the platform. That smart-looking man is a commercial traveller, and is too used to journeyings to be in the least daunted by the confusion. Not a bad companion if you are inclined to talk. He will tell you about the markets, about the bills he had returned on the fourth of the month, about the way in which he secures his customers. If for a few minutes he leaves off talking shop, and goes into politics, he will give you a hash of the leading articles he read to-day and yesterday. We are not describing the best, or even the second-best, but the average commercial traveller. When a commercial traveller is a man of education, he at once sinks the shop, and is as amusing a companion as the barrister crammed with circuit anecdotes. Near our commercial stands a county magnate. He is giving instructions to his servant about the luggage. Do not travel with him if you want to talk. If you are acquainted with him it would be all right, for he is well informed and full of gossip, but he never converses with strangers beyond offering a few observations on the state of the weather. Those two young men who are pacing the platform as noisily as possible are an apt illustration of the mercy of Providence. Their style of dress is slightly fast, and you can see that they are grandly aristocratic in their own opinion. Ten to one they are fledglings in her Majesty's Civil Service. Their father is an unfortunate barrister, or country parson, with a hundred and fifty a-year. He cannot afford to send them to the University, and they have not mettle enough in them to go forth and seek their fortune. So the father, who has good connections, gets them a nomination to the Civil Service, and, after much cramming, they pass the ordeal of examination. Unless by influence they will never rise to any other post than accrues to them by mere rotation. Yet see how the young men are comfortably blind to the actualities of their position. They have not the least idea that the maker of shoes is altogether a more independent workman than a Civil Service quill-driver. Not a word of this is intended as a reflection on the Civil Service. Some of the cleverest and hardest workers in the country are engaged in it. We merely refer to the C. S. ninnies, who are the drags and impediments of our public offices.

It is odd how easily one can tell by which class the people on the platform will travel. Those who can afford it do wisely in going first-class, and those who cannot afford first-class do stupidly in going second-class. The difference in comfort between the second and third class on English railroads is too homœopathic to be worth a brass farthing, and better people—we speak of long journeys—travel by third than by second class. That individual who is taking his family out of town is a shopkeeper. Likely enough he could afford first-class fare, but the expense is too much for his nerves. However, he is too genteel to go third-class, and so he will join the second-class " would be's !"

We shall avoid the carriage that fair maiden of thirty-five enters. As soon as she is seated, she will open her bag, take off her gloves, put her silver shield on one finger, and her thimble on another, and do fancy work. If the weather is oppressively hot, she will require the windows up, and if it is cold she will require the window down. Old maids are pleasant enough after forty, but from thirty to forty they are usually snappish. No wonder. Hope deferred has made the heart sick, and it is hard for them to reconcile themselves to the thought that their existence is to be a blank—a mere waste. Of course we shall not be so foolish as to be shut up with that fond mamma and her little ones. The young ladies in hats, with light literature in their hands—which they will not read—will be pleasant enough for those who know them, but we shall not enter their carriage. The etiquette of society is necessarily and properly strict, and all ladies who are worth talking with are not companionable unless duly introduced.

The third-class passengers are generally conspicuous from the ample supply of provisions that they carry with them in baskets. That aged couple are knee-deep in the fidgets. They have been to London to visit their married son, and are glad to go away from such a noisy place. How helpless they seem, and indeed how helpless they are! They are in everybody's way. They worry the porters with incessant questions about their luggage, and they are asking everyone on the platform which is their train. We really do not wish to be unkind to our provincial fellow-subjects, but it must be admitted that they are rather a nuisance in London, unless moving about under efficient guidance. The same remark, by the way, applies to your genuine Cockney in the country.

Ten minutes to one o'clock, and here is the train. We must be off for our ticket. After much squeezing, we get to the paying place. We are directed by an inscription on the counter to examine our tickets and change before leaving the counter, which, with the present ten minutes' arrangement, is an impossibility. We show our ticket to the porter, who is appointed to look after our luggage, and are informed that it is already in the van. We hope so, but it is in vain to attempt to get any ocular proof of the safety of our chattels.

What are the people staring at? Oh, there is an invalid carriage being attached to the train. That is all. Is it worth while to behold the scene for a moment? Lying on the bed, attended by mother and sister, and nurse, is a young girl, looking intently and lovingly at her father, who is standing by the carriage. What is the matter with her? She does not seem very ill—that is, not to those who know not how one fell disease veils its votaries with what is readily mistaken for the appearance of health. How white is her skin, and how clear is her complexion! Her eyes are lustrous and dilated. Her cheeks are flushed. She has just had some stimulant, after the exertion of moving. But, ah! that thin hand, lying on the cloak, with the fingers nervously twitching at the fringe, how it tells of wasting consumption! She is ordered to the sea-side. The physician did not say it would restore her, but he said it was the last chance of recovery. The father glares at us almost savagely. What right have we to peer into the carriage? How dare we say by a look of sympathy that we think his child is dying? Forgive us, for we respect your sorrow. We will intrude no more, not even by a glance at the carriage. Whilst there is life there is hope. May the light of your home not be turned to blackest darkness! May your darling be restored to health and strength by the sea breezes! May the order of nature not be inverted! Instead of your closing her dying eyes, may she in years to come wipe the perspiration from your brow when you are dying, and by her loving kindness mitigate in some degree the agony of the last mortal struggle!

We get into our carriage, and secure a corner seat. It will yet be three minutes before the second bell rings and the train starts. A long three minutes. How long it must have been to the father watching his sick child! How, no doubt, he prayed for the parting that he so much dreaded!

There is nothing more harrowing than the seconds that immediately precede the separation from those we love. Courage, brave father, for already two minutes out of the three belong to the eternity of the past. Don't let your breaking heart cause a muscle of your face to quiver. Smile as though you were glad and confident, for the doctor warned you not to dispirit your child. Courage, too, for the mother's sake, and for the sake of the trembling sister. But you must not attempt to speak. The choking lump in your throat would impede your utterance, and betray your emotion.

There is the whistle, and we are off in a moment. But the father cannot abide for that last moment. At the first sound of the whistle he turns suddenly from the carriage, and will not see the train move from the platform. He did what he could, he acted like a true man, but there is a limit to human endurance. When the hoarse screech of the engine proclaimed the instant of departure, all the agony of the last few hours was renewed and concentrated in a moment. The father had been thinking of the early days—of the early days when that child, the first-born, was the pet on which father and mother bestowed their fondest love. How she grew from day to day in stature and in beauty, and in sensibility! As she entered upon girlhood, how almost inordinate became the affection, and how jealous he felt of every one who seemed to love her! When she has been sick, how great has been his anxiety, and how deep his rejoicing when the sickness had passed away? How carefully she has been trained, and how well she has repaid all the care bestowed upon her! Well may her father be proud of her. And now that the time of harvest has come—now that for nineteen years the love of this child has been growing in his heart, she is perhaps to . . . Oh, let us not think of the little word that implies the loss of all these fond expectations. And all these recollections swept over the father like a torrent, and at the very last moment he was forced to retreat. He dared not give her the parting kiss that he had intended. He had borne himself like a hero, and then he turned away to look stern and haggard as he walked through the streets, and to weep like a little child when he reached his solitary home. Perhaps, in his solitude, the bereaved father will remember, that sad as the parting, it is the indispensable herald to the joys of meeting, and that the saddest of all partings is but the forerunner of that meeting of which the joy is inexpressible and everlasting.

Does a train ever leave a London station unladen with heavy hearts? and without leaving behind those who have found it impossible to utter the words "good bye," which signify "God be with you?" If you want to be cheerfully entertained at a railway station, do not spend an hour on the departure platform, but pass the hour on the arrival platform, where there are not sad partings, but joyful meetings.

A CHRISTMAS VISION.

———o———

ON a Christmas Day, not long ago, I found myself quite unexpectedly in the dining-room of my dear Aunt Letty. It was years since I had eaten my Christmas dinner with her, and, indeed, it was years since I had seen her. But there she was, as in the olden time, dressed in a gorgeous black velvet gown, and on her head one of those jaunty caps which I defy any modern milliner to rival. My aunt was one of those persons whose hearts never grow old. She was always merry, and everybody liked her. She was, as usual, looking a little worn with the cares of the season. My aunt's Christmas dinner was an institution, and, as I always thought, the acme of perfection. Is there any wonder that the good soul should look anxious? Suppose the stuffing balls in the soup should be underdone, or that the jugged hare should taste too strongly of the port wine, or that the tongue should be hard, or that the breast of the turkey should be disproportionately small, or that the joint of roast beef should not be so fine a cut as usual, or that the plum-pudding, gaily decorated with "Christmas," should refuse to come to the table in flames, or that the mince-pies should be somewhat sodden, or that the ripe old Stilton should not repay the care and wine bestowed upon it! Poor Aunt Letty, how overwhelming would have been her grief if any one of these catastrophes had happened! Besides my aunt's, there were many familiar faces in the room. My aunt had been a widow for a quarter of a century, and for nearly all that period had been engaged to one of the stoutest-hearted and best of men. From my childhood I had known Mr.

Tucker, and vividly remember the bright new shillings he used to give me. I think he must have had a contract with the Mint for a supply of new-coined money; at least, that was the conclusion which we sapient children arrived at. Dear old fellow, how cordially he greeted me, and how pleasantly he talked of "Auld Lang Syne!" He would do justice to my aunt's dinner. Of course Miss Titters was there. Oh, admirable Miss Titters! A very little lady, and mind to match, and a very little heart, but all of it good. Miss Titters was an old, old friend of the family, and quite one of ourselves. She was a maiden lady, I think nearly as old as my aunt, but she dressed like a girl, and I am angry now to think how unkindly I have sneered at so small and amiable a weakness. With her mincing walk, her mincing laugh, and her mincing talk, she always beguiled a pleasant five minutes. She had a cousin who was a captain, not a volunteer captain, but who had been a generation ago in his Majesty's service, and this Captain Bolton was the staple of her conversation. Miss Titters, no doubt, had degenerated a little from passing the best years of her life in boarding houses, but I cannot now recollect any of her faults—I only remember her affectionately, as one link of that long chain which binds me to a happy and never-to-be-forgotten past. Mr. Skirrow, our facetious companion, was in most excellent spirits. His jokes were not new nor original. We had heard them times and times out of number, but I am persuaded there never were before such good jokes uttered. He told with immense humour the story of his Irish friend who was informed before going to bed that a negro was stopping in the hotel and whose face was mischievously blackened after he fell asleep, and who being called by the waiter just in time to save the coach, looked in the glass, saw his dark countenance, rang the bell violently, shouted to the waiter he had called the negro, and besought him to call the right man, or he should be too late. Mr. Skirrow had a sneaking kindness for Miss Titters, and the sneaking kindness was reciprocated. There was a great deal of real sentiment vented when they bantered each other about celibacy. It would need a small volume to give the portraits of all who sat down to my aunt's dinner that day; but I am sure they had this in common, that in their hearts was not a drop of bitterness. Likely enough each one had a foe, but at that time there was no thought of enmity, and if the trespasses of each one were forgiven as each one forgave the trespassers against him, it was indeed a sinless party.

At the appointed hour we gathered at the table, which Mr. Skirrow always called the "festive board," although it was of the best mahogany. If my dear little aunt appreciated praises, she had her desire. The soup was superlative. The jugged hare—my aunt was very proud of her jugged hare—was as perfect a production of the culinary art as ever delighted the human palate. The breast of the turkey was gigantic, and white as the driven snow. The tongue was as soft as butter. The roast beef was worthy of old England. The pudding was worthy of my aunt, and the mince pies were wonderfully puffy. My aunt, dear old-fashioned soul, had no new-fangled notions about French wines, and her port and sherry were incomparable. It was a custom at her dinner-table for the guests to drink to each other, and everybody drank with everybody else over and over again, before the Stilton, in a beautiful state of mouldiness, made its appearance. Then the cloth is drawn, not one cloth, but both, and on the mahogany, shining like a mirror, is placed the dessert. A glass of wine all round to the health of our hostess. The glasses were full to the brim, but not so full as our hearts. Aunt Letty smiled, and soon after took off her spectacles and wiped them with her handkerchief. Then Mr. Tucker returned thanks for my aunt, getting rather thick and husky when he spoke of her goodness, and wound up by giving the toast of "Absent friends." Mr. Skirrow gave his annual toast, "The single married, and the married happy," to which Miss Titters drank with trepidation. Mr. Muggins, who was the fast man of the party, and who told grand tales during the dinner about the rehearsal of the pantomime at the theatre on Christmas eve—how the stage-manager could not get the supernumeraries to attend to their work—how he (Mr. Muggins) got up a little flirtation with one of the ballet-girls—how the musical director had *invented* stunning comic tunes by playing Scotch psalms in double quick time—proposed in an elaborate speech, which he arose to deliver under difficulties, the time-honoured toast of "The Ladies." These and many others being responded to, the singing commenced. Aunt Letty protested that she was too old; but we could not bear that. Aunt Letty grow old, and not able to sing! After a very little persuasion she warbled, with a degree of feeling which more than compensated for every artistic imperfection, and for the wear and tear of years, the old ballad of "Sally in our Alley;" Mr. Tucker obliged us with "The Friar in Orders Grey;" Mr. Skirrow essayed a sentimental ballad, and it was fortunate for him that his audience were friendly. Miss Titters was evidently affected by Mr. Skirrow's song, for she was silent for nearly five minutes, which was altogether an unprecedented incident in her history.

But I must hasten on with my story. Like a vision it seems to me now, and must be told briefly. The singing over, the tables are cleared away, and the party sits down to "Pope Joan." A splendid round game is "Pope Joan,"—speculation enough in it, and plenty of occasions for mirth. What a laugh when Mr. Skirrow got "Intrigue!" What a shout when Miss Titters got "Matrimony!"

I did not join the card-table. I sat apart, I know not why, and looked on. I sympathised with the happiness around me, but yet partook not of it. Between me and all earthly happiness there was a dark cloud, which no sunshine of merriment could dispel. By-and-by I noticed that there was some whispering at the round table, and that ever and anon my loving friends looked towards me. At length there came a loud sonorous knock at the door. The game was stopped. My aunt threw down the cards, came to me, and putting her hand upon my shoulder, said, "She has come at last, and now you will be happy."

And whilst she was yet speaking there came into the room she who was my world and my hope. I felt utterly bewildered. And she came to me as in days gone by, kissed me as though we had been parted for hours and not for years, and smiled as though she knew not that my heart was breaking with a joy that could not be uttered. Quite unchanged was my darling, and in all the beauty of her girlhood. There was no tracing of care or sorrow on her face, and she looked calm and sweetly joyful as of yore.

Let me try in a few words to describe her, only, alas! to realise how utterly impossible it is to convey by words any impression of her loveliness. A slim girlish figure. Her head perfectly formed. Her hair always wild, and finer than the finest silken tresses ever dreamt of. Not dark, yet seeming so when contrasted with the paleness of her brow. Her forehead large, yet in beautiful harmony with the rest of her features. Her eyes dark, liquid, and ever talking more eloquently than tongue can do. Her mouth was not formed according to rules of art, and yet was passing pretty. But it was not her features. Those, indeed, might be painted or chiselled, but it was the countenance, the æsthetical beauty, which may be felt, but cannot be portrayed. It was singularly animated, and yet singularly placid. It was mingled sunshine and starlight. It was like unto the incarnate expression of religious ecstacy. It was a heavenly glow, the manifestation of the inner divinity, the reflection of her pure and holy spirit. If I write like a lover, I have an excuse. None saw her without loving her, and all who read this sketch, and knew her, will wonder why I write so coldly of one who was the material type of those brightest dreams which inspire men in the heyday of their first and only love. And let me add that her character was not less beautiful. A flirt, I think, she had been—nay, I know she had been a flirt—and yet not one thought of evil had entered into her mind. So guileless in her prattle, so innocent in her opinions, she thought kindly of all mankind; and her noble frankness, her spotless truthfulness—for no falsehood had ever polluted her lips — were a complete armour to her, and she passed through the ordeal of life unscathed.

Aunt Letty having kissed us both, went back to the table, and the game was renewed. I think her stock of fishes must have been much reduced by negligence, for she was continually looking towards us, and nodding at me, as much as to say, "Be happy now." I was supremely happy. My darling was leaning her head upon me, and her hand was grasped in mine. The first words I spoke were to ask her if she would leave me again; and she raised her head from my shoulder, and shook it in a manner peculiar to her, and smiled. And the assurance that she would not leave me gave me delight that I never experienced before, and never can again.

Who has not realised how true, even as an allegory, is the Biblical description of the fall of man? Who forgets the Paradise of Childhood? Who forgets those days when the terrors of mortality were unknown, and when there was no consciousness of sin? Alas! that the joys of the Paradise of Childhood so soon pass away. We eat of the tree of knowledge, and we are driven forth from that Garden of Eden. Try what we will, or how we will, we can return to it no more, except by the dark valley of the shadow of death. Yet is the desert of life not all dreary. There are oases in it, where for a little while we rest and gather strength for the journey that is before us, unto the land of unbroken rest. It was just such an interval of surpassing peace that I was blessed with that Christmas night, when my darling—mine, then, oh my darling, and mine for ever and ever—was by my side.

Presently, Aunt Letty came again to us, and kissing us both, said, " You had better go now, and I will say good night for you." The next incident I remember was being with my darling in a railway-carriage. It was the depth of winter, and yet not a wintry night. The moon shone brightly, a few stars were glittering, and vieing with the moonlight, and as we sped along we could see the green fields and the leafless trees, and no more beautiful panorama could be looked upon. By-and-by our journey was completed, and we walked to a loved trysting-place on the banks of the Thames. I recollect it was high-water, and the river, luminous with the moonlight, flowed on, amidst a surrounding silence almost oppressive. And I said to my darling, "Oh, if we could die now!" and she replied, "Dear one, I do not believe in death, now or ever—rather let us talk of life." The silent river became a thing of dread to me, and I was seized with a strange, wild impulse to cast myself into it. I was conscious that my brain was on fire, and that the tumult of joy had almost dethroned reason. I said to my darling, "Promise never to leave me, never to leave me," and she replied, "Never, never! let us go and register the vow before God." Just then I heard the sound of church bells, and I was amazed, for it was night. My darling took my hand in hers. We passed swiftly across the bridge; we passed the red brick edifice that was once the residence of kings, we crossed the green, we entered through a path that I had never traversed before, into the midst of the park, and then we came upon a chapel. As we went in, my darling whispered to me, "It is the festival of the Nativity." The chapel was almost in darkness, and the moonlight streamed through the coloured windows. Even the altar was so dimly lighted that we could discern nothing save the white vestments of the priests. Yet one perceived with curious contradictory distinctness all the decorations. The red berries and the mistletoe, the red and white camelias and the devices formed with the flowers were visible to us. There was the odour of incense. After a season of summer heat, when a shower falls, the earth yields a rich perfume — its sacrifice of thanksgiving for the refreshing rain. The incense that pervaded the chapel reminded me of this perfume. The choristers were singing that part of the "Te Deum" which recites the glory and the work of the Saviour. The peculiarity of the music was that every note seemed pregnant with thought. Nay, the music had power to give acute physical pain, and exuberant physical pleasure. As the words "Sharpness of death" were uttered with a sort of kissing scream, the hearer suffered a mortal agony. Every nerve tingled with pain so that a prolongation of that outcry would have been unbearable. It passed away, and the memory of it was swallowed up in the triumphant shout with which choir and organ proclaimed that Christ has opened the "Kingdom of Heaven to all believers." The holly and the flowers with which the chapel was covered from the ground to the roof, rustled, and, as it were, echoed the notes of praise. The prayers were over, and a priest stood at the foot of the altar and began to preach. Then followed an episode never to be forgotten. He seemed not to speak, and yet one felt he was speaking and knew what he said. Suddenly the altar became wrapt in a blaze of light. It was so dazzling that the eye quailed before it. I covered my face with my hands, but it was impossible to shut out the light. It flashed through the closed eyelids, and seemed to enter through every pore of the skin. My darling put her hand upon mine, and I opened my eyes and looked towards the altar.

In the midst of the glory about the altar there appeared in endless perspective a picture of that memorable scene of the shepherds watching their flocks by night, and of the heavens opening, and of a multitude of angels, that could not be numbered, singing the glorious anthem of "Peace on earth, good-will to man." I remember being struck with the non-Oriental appearance of the landscape, though the shepherds were draped in a loose garment, and with sandals on their feet. I was still more surprised to hear the angelic host sing the anthem of peace and good-will. Excited and thrilled as my mind was, I could still reason upon what was passing. I could not understand by what device angels in the picture were apparently made to sing. The pictures, which take minutes to describe, came and vanished like a flash of lightning, and it was remarkable that in the instant the whole subject was unfolded, and even an anthem sung. The picture of the announcement of the Nativity faded away, and in place of it we beheld a multitude of men and women and little children crowding about one who stood upon a gentle eminence with a glory around his head, and he stretched forth his hands to the right and to the left, and as he did so we could see that the men, and the women, and the children were filled with gladness. The scene changes. A dark, drear, and wasted plain appears. On a little hill is a representation of the Crucifixion. There was a gloom that appeared almost sensible to the touch, and there reigned an awful silence. Again the scene changes. We see a cave, and in it lying a dead man. By the side of the corpse was Death, hideous figure, seated on his pale horse, watching intently the face of the dead man. Above the cave, and high in the heavens, there appeared standing a host of angels, with their harps by their side, and their crowns at their feet, and they seemed to tremble and quake exceedingly. There was a pause. Grim Death leered triumphantly. There was a shout, as it were, from the throats of a myriad of demons—"Who can resist thy sting? thou hast gotten the victory." And the angels appeared still more exceedingly to tremble and quake. Another pause. Slowly arose the dead man. With a horrid screech, echoed by the myriad demons, Death fled on his pale horse, and there was a shout of triumph which drowned the cry of despair. The angels, with the noise of ten thousand thousand trumpets, exclaimed, "Oh, death, where is thy sting—Oh, grave, where is thy victory?" Then the angels were crowned again, and, taking their harps, they sang "Hallelujah, hallelujah, to the Lamb of God!"

The glory faded from the altar, but there was no more darkness, and I looked round upon my darling, and I was surprised to see her dressed as a bride. The priest came from the altar to where we were kneeling. He placed my hand in hers, and said, "God has joined you, and no man can part you." I put my arms about her, and I felt her hot breath upon my face as she kissed me. I said to her, "Oh, darling wife, this joy is too great, what shall I do—what shall I do?" I seemed to be falling; I felt faint; I felt that the faintness of death was upon me, when

* * * * * * * * *

There is a knock at my door.

I awoke—it is Christmas morning. Not that day did I forget, nor yet in days to come shall I forget the Christmas vision. Never in any days to come shall I cease to remember vividly—and to love, passionately—my sweet Christmas wife. The vision, indeed, was unreal in many respects; but as to her beauty, her goodness, and her love, it was true. Ah, my sweet wife, I forget not what you said to me as we stood by the river. Ah, my darling, ever in my loneliness I am not alone. Neither, darling, do I believe in death, now or ever. Whom God hath joined, Death cannot part.

A BREEDING ESTABLISHMENT.

It was raining, as it had been doing, with brief intervals of fog, for three or four months. As we—the "we" stands in this case for self and friend—as we sped along in a comfortable railway carriage, the prospect was anything but cheering. We were bound for a breeding establishment, and the idea of walking about wet paddocks was not exhilarating. Our friend, who was smoking with the connivance of the guard, was inclined to temper dyspepsia, and indulged in the dreariest of puns and the gloomiest of prognostications. He remarked that the weather was like the Queen, always "reigning," and *apropos* of the greenness of the grass, observed that last year we had no keep for cattle, and this year he supposed we should have any quantity of keep and no cattle. We suggested that, under the circumstances, we should have to take our animal food first hand, and we told him the story of the Irishman who consulted a London physician. Says the son of Escalapius, "Take plenty of animal food, and that will put you right." About a week later Paddy paid a second visit to the doctor, looking worse than before. "Sure, doctor," said he, "I tried to do what you told me. I managed the beans and the oats pretty well, but the hay and the chaff were too much for me. I could not get them down raw, and even when fried in butter the stomach was as obstinate as a pig." "Why, man alive, what made you try to eat beans and oats, and hay and chaff?" "Why," says Paddy, scratching his head, "sure your honour told me to take plenty of 'animal food.'" Even this stale and feeble joke was acceptable on such a day, and it led to others quite as feeble, which whiled away the time until we arrived at our destination. Here we met the gentleman—he really is a jolly good fellow — who was to chaperon us over the establishment. This gentleman has an alarming knowledge of what the professors in London schools and colleges call equinatics. He knows the descent of English race-horses for at least two centuries. With horses blood is everything. A shopkeeper may be the father of a Lord Chancellor, but a cart-horse will never be the sire of a Derby winner. As the "Master"—that is the name the stablemen call him—as the Master observed, "Horses do not run with their heads or with their blood, but they cannot run without them."

The first business was to refresh at the Master's house, which is a charming place even on a soaking day. Just large enough to be comfortable, and surrounded by paddocks that looked from the windows as carefully mowed as the Slopes at Windsor. . Whilst drinking some sherry—none of your free-trade stuff, that is only good for the druggists and undertakers—we had a glance at the picture gallery. There were portraits of horses yet in the flesh, and of horses that were in the flesh when Black, and Watts, and Newcomen were gestating the iron horse. For the moment there seemed to us to be very little in these equine portraits—we are not horsey—but on closer inspection, and with the assistance of the Master, we perceived that, to use his forcible illustration, there is as much difference between horses as there is between women. Having taken several glasses of sherry, but leaving off with a wholesome thirst for more—a butt of it does not contain a single headache—we set out for the stables. Before doing so, our friend whose spirits were wonderfully revived by the sherry, thrust a bottle of gin into his pocket. As a rule, stablemen are not addicted to teetotalism, but rather incline the other way; and our friend wisely assumed that the bottle of gin would be a welcome guest, cheer the heart and loosen the tongue.

Across the paddocks to the saddle-room—so denominated, we suppose, because a few saddles and bridles are hung about the walls. It is in reality the parlour, kitchen, and hall of the stablemen. The room we entered is like a stable without stalls, and furnished like a tap-room, minus the pots, spittoons, and sanded floor. A kitchen-range, with a roaring fire, a wooden table, built for strength, and not for show, three benches around the fire, and a something in the corner which is probably a truckle bedstead. Withal a neat and clean room, for cleanliness and tidiness are as much insisted on in a breeding establishment as in a Belgravian nursery. There were three stablemen in the room. They were sitting staring at the fire, in that condition of physical, and apparently mental, composure that is peculiar to their class. Ned, the eldest, was a wiry-looking customer. As a youngster he had been famous for his capacity for eating. He had been backed against a Birmingham man for a large sum of money to out-eat him. The food selected was giblet-pie and bread, and the contest began at 8 a.m. At 11 o'clock the backers of Ned were informed that their man was half a giblet-pie and a quartern loaf a-head. At 2 o'clock Ned was two pies and two loaves a-head, when the Brum gave up the contest, and Ned emptied a basin of sugar, just to show that his wonderful appetite was not materially impaired by the morning's work. He is no longer the man he was, for now a pound of steak for breakfast, and a pork-pie for lunch, takes the sharp edge off his appetite. Tom was rather more fleshy than Ned, and enjoyed a joke immensely. His noisy laugh was a cross between a horse's neigh and an ordinary human laugh. Bill was a smartish young man, who from his youth upwards had been the nurse, guide, and friend, of a celebrated stallion. All three had short-cropped, and very greasy hair, enormous shawls round their throats, fastened with conspicuous pins, and horsified trowsers—that is, trowsers fitting closely to the legs and ancles.

Having seated ourselves by the fire, on the aforesaid

benches, the conversation began about the weather. Ned did not remember such a season since Redbeard was foaled, and that was twenty years ago. Tom opined that it was a wetter winter when Shandygaff died from strangles. Here the Master chimed in with an anecdote. Walking down the main street in Newmarket on a rainy night, he met a jockey, and remarked that " Jupiter Pluvius was coming down." "Ah!" exclaimed the jockey, "what are they laying agin 'im ?" Our stable companions laughed, as in duty bound, at the Master's anecdote, but they did not see the fun of it. They appeared much more intelligent when the Master proposed a damper, and the bottle of gin was brought forth. A broken fork was substitute for a corkscrew. Glasses were not to be had, but there were two teacups and two tin pannikins. The kettle was boiling, and the grog was mixed. Ned would not partake of it, as he abjured spirits, and stuck to strong ale, so he joined us in a cup of tea. Pretty good tea, taken from a paper packet with the fingers, and put into a teapot nearly as black as the kettle. The only sugar to be had for tea or grog was brown sugar, and that peculiarly sandy. There was only one spoon. Tom, who was drinking with Bill, stirred the grog with his pipe, which, we should imagine, gave an additional flavour to the gin-and-water.

Ned being informed by the Master that we were green, and wanted to know a little about breeding, gave us an account of the business, which was not particularly lucid or connected. It seems, however, that the offspring of aristocratic horses get more care than is bestowed on the majority of the children of men. The dams, the sires, and the foals are watched night and day; their tempers are studied; they are well fed, and every attention is bestowed upon the development of their strength. If they are in the slightest degree indisposed the doctor is sent for, and if the patient is seriously ill the groom must remain up with his charge all night. Not that it is any hardship, for the stablemen love their horses; and when we had seen them, we understood, and fully excused the fondness. Ned said they had been very lucky this year, as they had a crack foal on the 2nd of January. Why was that lucky? Bless our innocent eyes!

The Master explained to us that the age of race-horses dates from the 1st of January. A horse born on the 31st of December, 1865, would be in the racing record a year old on the 1st of January, 1866; whereas, a horse born on the 1st of January, 1866, would not be a year old until the 1st of January, 1867. As horses compete as two-year olds, it is all-important to get them foaled as soon after the 1st of January as possible; and to be foaled in December is fatal to a racing career.

"Ah," said Tom, "that was a queer start of old Muggins. It was in this here way. A mare was horrid for'ard soon arter Christmas, and she were the crack of the stable. Old Muggins were in a sweat, and how he does pray and swear that the mare might not tumble to pieces afore the fust! Well, about nine o'clock on the 31st—leastways, it were about nine o'clock by the church-clock—the mare foaled. Old Muggins calls I and tother chap into his room and wishes us a happy new year. He gives us a drop o' grog and says, with never so much as a wink, that it were jolly that the mare did not foal afore morning. This gives I and tother chap a start. I says, 'the mare aint foaled an hour.' 'Well,' said old Muggins, 'what's the time?' We said it were about ten. 'Yer be blowed,' said he, 'just come and look at my clock.' So me and tother chap did, and I am blessed if his clock warnt three o'clock. In course there was no disputing that there, and the foal was registered according."

The Master remarked that Tom was as smart as old Muggins, and made a pound or two outside the regular wages.

"Yes," chimed in Ned, "so do we, but *we* does it on the square. "Whoever brings mares here get summut, and whoever's turn it is to take them home gets a summut."

"Tom, how do you manage the touts in your part of the country?" asked the Master.

"All square." replied Tom, "Them there gents comes a-prowling about the place to get a summut for to send to the papers. Now, Master, we must not tell nothing about the stables, and we don't. This is what we does. We stuffs 'em with lies. So we gets their tin, and we don't break no rules. I can't read myself, more can Ned, but Bill can, and how we chuckles when we hears of our fibbing tips which we have planted on the tipsters."

The great idea in breeding, so far as we can understand, seems to be: firstly, to select a well-bred and symmetrical mare; and, secondly, to put her to one of the most fashionable sires of the day. The produce is almost sure to command a large price. If, to talk "stable," "it does not turn out a parson, it will make a clerk," or, in other words, if it proves useless as a racehorse, you have still the blood, which may again be made available for breeding purposes.

Mares early in the year are for the most part in an interesting condition, which, as a matter of course, necessitates the greatest care, attention, and judicious management.

When a mare is about to foal, she is removed to a box provided for the purpose, with hot water and other appliances ready, in case of materfamilias having "a hard time of it;" whilst a groom is always at hand to officiate as nurse, should such services be required—comparatively speaking, a rarity. In ordinary cases nature does its work, and the mare, who almost invariably foals in the night, is found in the morning "pretty comfortable," and the precocious foal on its legs taking nourishment.

Foaling time is a "trying time" for the stud groom, who is right glad when he is enabled to furnish Messrs. Weatherby with a correct return of the current year's produce for the stud-book.

In May or June the yearlings are sold, sent to their

trainer's quarters to be broken in, and are at once engaged for two and three year old stakes, according to the estimate formed of their abilities by their new owners.

After much instructive and facetious conversation, we left the saddle-room to have a look at the horses—beginning with the stallions. Each of these valuable creatures —worth from £3,000 to £10,000—has a separate establishment. A gate is unbarred and unlocked, and we enter the straw-yard reserved for the use of the horse which, as real names need not be mentioned, we will call the Prince. A comfortable yard for exercise when the paddocks are not in a fit condition. Rising above the walls, which are eight feet high, is a wooden partition, for Prince is playful, and was in the habit of putting his front hoofs on the top of the wall and looking over, to the imminent danger of injuring his costly carcase. Tom unlocks the stable door, and we stand in the presence of Prince. We see the reasonableness of padding your stable from floor to roof, sweet Prince! There you are snorting, prancing, and striking out your legs in a manner rather alarming to us. Tom assures us that you have no vice, and that you would not hurt a new-born baby. Perhaps not, but we do not wish to test your amiability by getting near to your hind legs. What is play to a groom is death to an unhorsified individual. We remember, Tom, the Master's story, about a groom who had to sell a—well, a playful—horse to a greenhorn. The greenhorn was informed that the animal was free from all tricks and vice. By-and-by the virtuous animal made a lunge with his leg, which fractured one of the groom's ribs. "Halloa!" said the greenhorn, "that looks like vice. Are you hurt?" The groom was equal to the occasion. "Hurt!" said he, smiling, "of course not. It is just the way with the playful dear to tickle me in the ribs, and it always makes my eyes water as if I had been a-rubbing them with onions." This clinched the business, and the playful horse and the confiding greenhorn were forthwith simultaneously sold. Tom having now stripped Prince, led him up to us.

Prince was disposed to be friendly, and evinced a desire to taste one of the buttons of our coat. We held a walking-cane in his mouth. Prince bit it with marked enjoyment. "Horses likes to bite a stick, sir," said Tom, "and they often has a grab at us, not 'cause they're ezactly vicious, but 'cause they are fond."

What on earth can we say about you, Prince? What words can do you justice? You are as beautiful as you were on the day you won the Derby. Your skin has upon it a glossiness almost dazzling, and yet beneath it, so fine is it, one can see the veins through which your proud blood is coursing. It is some time since you won the Derby, but Time has forgotten to mark you. Your eye has not lost its brightness, your form is not less symmetrical, and you are, as of yore, fleet as the wind.

We stood at the further end of the stable in the spot selected by the skilful Master for a favourable view. What a neck! Curving just enough to lend grace to the haughtiness with which the head is raised, as it were, in defiance of all creation. It appeared to us that the Prince had a wonderfully broad back, but the Master told us that there was nothing unusual in its dimensions. Legs thin, but strong looking, and planted on the ground firmly. As for the thighs, it was wonderful to see how muscle was lapped over muscle.

A grand creature is Prince. Grand and beautiful and loveable. There are many of the humanities about a horse that appertain to no other quadruped. Lions and tigers may be very magnificent in the forest or in the jungle, but so, too, is the wild horse magnificent. Here is the difference. The horse becomes docile, but without losing any of its spirit. There is the caged lion, writhing under control. There is the horse, submitting to control without writhing, even as man,—that is, a wise and noble-spirited man—submits. The finer the breed, and the higher the spirit of the horse, the more submissive is he to lawful authority. Is it not so with man? Prince, old fellow, although you are a horse, are you not a sort of a brother? Come here, you pet! Steady, my darling. It is not the thing to hug you; but, sweet Prince, we are not professional. Our trowsers do not fit our calves like an extra skin. So we will even hug you round the neck.

Farewell, Prince. And very well you will fare; and you ought to fare well. What a hatfull of money you won for your owner during your racing career, and cups and plates enough to cover a goodly-sized sideboard! Now that your racing career is over, are you useless? Useless! Prince brings in from £2,000 to £3,000 a-year as a stud horse.

We looked at more stallions, at some mares and foals, and, finally, at the yearlings. The yearlings are separately stabled from the time of their being weaned in the autumn. At present they are rough in their coats—February is an unfavourable month for inspecting them—and timid before strangers, but are pretty things in their way. . This one is by Prince out of Princess, and was foaled in January last year. In about three months it will be sold, and its groom expects that it will fetch a thousand guineas! "Aye," says Ned, who looks after the young stock, "I wish my produce were worth the like." Yes, Ned, but you are not a philosopher. We grant you things are worth what they fetch, but depend upon it, Ned, some things are worth more than they will fetch. Your "kids"—that is the "stable" word for children—would not sell for much; but, after all, they are worth more than foals. Well, Ned, we agree with you so far as to hope that the day will come when the children of the poor will be as well housed as racing foals. But, Ned, we are not all born with a silver spoon in our mouth and with blue blood in our veins. Neither are all horses born equal. The hack foal has a hard time of it. Look at your London cab horse. Don't you remember, Ned, the Master's pitiable tale about the cab horse that died in the street from exhaustion? "Vell," exclaimed the cabman, "this comes of buyin' cheap 'osses. Ven I spekylates again I'll 'ave a good 'un, if I gives thutty bob for 'un."

In spite of Ned's sage opinion "that them are best off as has nothin' whatever to do wi' 'oss flesh," we have—since our visit—been awfully spoony on it, and read the sporting papers with a dangerous relish. We have even suggested to our tailor that our trowsers would be improved if they were a trifle tighter about the legs.

TWO MIDNIGHT MEETINGS.

———o———

"I should like to know for what, in the name of goodness, you brought the poor girls into the world, Mr. Gummer."

Mrs. Gummer was highly incensed. The Misses Gummer had received an invitation to a ball, and their papa had objected to their acceptance thereof on the score of expense. Perhaps he cannot afford it; but are his unfortunate offspring to suffer for the parental impecuniosity? Mrs. Gummer was aggravated at such mean, paltry, fiddle-faddle. Why did not Mr. Gummer rouse himself, and make a fortune as other men did? If Mrs. Gummer had been a man her daughters should not have been jeered and sneered at, and snubbed, and put upon by everybody. By hook or by crook she would have got money. But what does Mr. Gummer care? So long as his wants are satisfied his wife and children may be miserable, degraded, wretched creatures. Why did he take Mrs. Gummer from her happy home? For what did he bring the poor girls into the world?

Mr. Gummer was completely posed. He had been for years trying to find out why he had married Mrs. Gummer, and the only guess he could make was that he had done so in a fit of temporary insanity. As to the girls, he had brought them into the world without any particular views, or, indeed, without any views at all. But motive or no motive, the Misses Gummer are in the world, and the natural end and aim of their existence is marriage. But how are girls to get married unless they are sent to market? It is not their fault, pretty dears, that they are still on papa's hands. They go to a church where all the curates are unmarried; but curates do not place their affections on poor girls. At the sea-side the Misses Gummer have exhibited their charms on the afternoon parade; they have wandered about the sea-shore with their hair dishevelled after bathing, and they have gathered around themselves a host of devoted admirers. In vain their unremitting exertions. The cold-blooded fish, after nibbling at the bait, and sporting with the fair anglers, have swum away. But the church and the sea-shore are outside places. The ball-room is the legitimate and best hymeneal market. There dress and wine, seductive music, and exciting dances combine to throw batchelors off their guard, and to allure them to propose. Are the Misses Gummer to be kept from the market because their papa cannot afford to put them into marketable trim? Were they brought into the world to be disgusting old maids? Mr. Gummer relents. Better let his creditors suffer than his children. As Mrs. Gummer often tells him, " a man who does not care for his own household is worse than an infidel." Confound the creditors!

Mrs. Gummer is by no means extravagant: that is, she makes a great show at a comparatively small cost. The Misses Gummer will look "howling swells" for a mere trifle. Provided it is silk with a good face, what does it signify about the quality of the stuff? Who under tarlatan can tell the difference between a 1s. 11½d. silk and a 4s. 6d. silk? Plenty of petticoats to make the skirt set out, and a handsome-looking ball-dress, bodice included, can be purchased for a trifle under three pounds, and, moreover, the same slip and bodice will last for nearly a season. Gloves do not come out of papa's pocket. The Misses Gummer do a little betting, and their wagers are always for gloves. When they lose they do not pay, and when they win they invariably choose white gloves, for a good kid will dye well, and be—except for the smell—equal to new. Boots are rather expensive, but they last for some time. Well rubbed with bread crumbs they can be kept in a state of demisemi-whiteness for many occasions; and when they will no longer clean they may be blackened with ink, and serve for those minor occasions when it is not indispensable for the feet to be shod in white satin.

Shortly after ten the Misses Gummer, under the escort of their fond mamma, arrive at their friend's house, partake of a cup of tea in the ante-room, and ascend to the ball-room, biting their lips by the way, not from vexation, but to make them appear very red. For awhile the entertainment is somewhat dreary and depressingly slow. The young men seem half afraid to approach the vestals, and dance with a stiffness that is more decorous than exhilarating. The first quadrille is solemn, the first polka is methodical, the performance of the "Lancers," would delight a dancing-master, and during the first waltz the gentlemen arm their partners without cuddling them. Conversation is forced, jerky, and flat. The vestals remark that the room is rather cold, and their cavaliers agree with them. The gentlemen criticise the music favourably, and the fair ones endorse the criticism. There is a little chat about the sea-side and the Rhine; but it is a painful effort. However, by midnight the room is warm, the guests are lively, and there is no more formality. The before-supper polka is danced with loud enjoyment and casino ease. The berthas of the vestals and the shirt fronts of the gentlemen are in touching proximity. The cavaliers pant compliments, to which the vestals respond with speaking glances. Sweet and impressive scene! The gentlemen are clad in half-mourning for their sins, and the ladies are so clad, that though they may not be able to attain to the innocency of Eve before the fall, yet they are manifestly determined, as far as they can, to attain to the nakedness of Eve in a state of innocency. Their bodices are designed to reveal those charms which in a puritanical age it was deemed modest to conceal. The discreet mammas, who know their cue, do not attempt by their presence to check the flow of affection, but —prudent dames!—have already, with a few of the papas, made their way to the supper-room, and are busy with the best parts of the cold fowl.

Miss Cecilia Gummer is taken down to supper by Charles Softly, who is rather "green," and who has expectations. The more astute ones remark that "Charley is awfully spoony," and the vestals are disgusted that the young man should be so taken with the creature in pink tarlatan. It is a stand-up supper, and Charley has ample opportunities for exhibiting his devotion. With a tenderness that is really affecting he turns over the pile of fowl till he comes to a piece of the breast, for no other part of the bird would be worthy to enter the stomach of the fair Cecilia. When he hands her a glass of wine he is repaid a million-fold for his trouble by the sweet smile that is bestowed upon him. The jelly and blanc-mange are agitated when he hands them to her. Charley is so enchanted that he positively gives Cecilia some trifle without the accustomed joke. What a good, kind, disinterested girl Cecilia is! She absolutely thinks that men have something else to do in life besides waiting upon women. She beseeches Mr. Softly to take some supper. This unprecedented condescension was almost too much for Charley. He could hardly restrain the impulse to flop down on his knees before the assembled guests. He relieved himself by pulling a *bon-bon* with Cecilia, and, after the slight explosion, he read to her the following motto, which was wrapped round the sugar-plum :—

> Oh, dearest girl, my heart is thine,
> Shall we for e'er our fates combine?
> If you reject my proffered suit,
> For ever shall this tongue be mute.

The next motto was even more sublime :—

> Thine eyes, fair maid, have fired my heart,
> I burn to clasp thee to my breast;
> I am undone if we must part—
> Oh! deign to make my passion blest!

The sounds of a galop descend through the ceiling, and

the supper-room is soon cleared of all except the mammas and papas, who are the last to leave, as well as the first to come. When we are young we are anxious about the heart, and do not care about the stomach; but frequently after fifty we leave the heart to take care of itself, and pay the utmost attention to the claims of the stomach. The after-supper galop is encored, and won't the legs that dance it suffer for the work next morning? Skirts are torn, couples knock against each other, beads of perspiration stand upon the brows of the gentlemen, the headgear of the ladies becomes disordered, and the conversation is decidedly noisy.

Before the galop is over Cecilia is exhausted, and her devoted Charley leads her into a conservatory attached to the drawing-room, which is lighted with coloured lamps, tastefully arranged. So exhausted is Cecilia that she is compelled to accept the support of Charley's arm around her waist, and Charley shakes as though he were made of *blanc-mange*, or was suffering from a fit of ague. We have said he was green, and this was, indeed, his first serious affair. He draws Cecilia nearer and nearer to him, and she, kind damsel, is not in the least coy. One arm is round her waist; with his disengaged hand he grasps her hand, and mutters, "Oh, Miss Gummer!" Fair Cecilia bends her head, and replies with a sigh, a gentle sigh, that would not disturb the tiniest atom of down that ever floated in the air. Charley is immensely excited, and he ventures to kiss fair Cecilia's forehead. "Oh, you naughty man," ejaculates the vestal, and she leans more heavily than before on the arm of Mr. Softly, and gives him one long look, not of reproach, but of angelic pity. Charley whispers, "Oh, Cecilia, I love you, may I hope you are not indifferent?" The tremulous response comes, "I cannot believe it, I don't know what to say." Just as if it was the first time she had gone through the ceremony! Charley hugs her to him and imprints a kiss upon her lips. "Oh, don't, pray don't," ejaculates the happy fair one. Charley, for his life's sake, beseeches her to say that she is not indifferent, and that he may have some hope. The vestal remembers that Mr. Softly has good expectations, and, therefore, hiding her blushing face on the bosom of her admirer, she confesses she is not quite indifferent. Charley is in ecstacies. In the delirium of his joy he kisses the fair and bare shoulder of Cecilia, and the modern Diana does not shrink from the ardent embrace. What a beautiful amalgamation of chastity and kindness! How charmingly, too, does Cecilia remember the exigencies of business in the excitement of pleasure. Only a few minutes are spent in the conservatory, yet the offer is made and accepted, and the hour is arranged at which the beatified lover shall see mamma in the morning. Cecilia is too wise to refer such a business to her papa.

Charley leaves the conservatory wild with delight. He has no idea, unsophisticated young man, that the virgin heart which he has just bought has been for may seasons, like an hotel, open to all comers.

A few more dances, in which Cecilia does not join, and the meeting is over. The jaded beauties get into their carriages, and are driven home. Those who have received offers, or at least such attentions as promise to lead to offers, are happy and contented. Those who have not been successful are unreasonably discontented. When the buyers are few, and the supply of stock is large, it is not to be expected that every fair one offered will find a purchaser. Courage, courage, my dear girls! Condescend to learn patience even from the records of Smithfield. At that great mart the creatures that are passed by one day are advantageously disposed of at a future marketing.

*　　*　　*　　*　　*　　*　　*

On the same night, not far from the same place, there is another midnight meeting. It is held at a public place of entertainment—a lecture-hall. Fifty or sixty girls in bonnets and walking attire are present. About a dozen gentlemen, the majority of them ministers of the Gospel, are handing about refreshments, and the air is strongly impregnated with the philanthropic odour produced by the combined fumes of tea, coffee, and hot muffins. The girls are for the most part pretty and well-dressed, though a few are poorly clad. There is a great deal of whispering going on, and some laughter, but it is that kind of laughter which comes from the throat, and which is resorted to, not because the heart is glad, but to conceal sadness. Presently the gentlemen assemble on a platform at the end of the room, and a short prayer is offered up. Two or three of the girls bend their heads—the rest sit bolt upright, smiling at each other, and looking ever and anon defiantly towards the platform. When the prayer is over, one of the ministers stands up to speak. He is a venerable-looking man, with an earnest, kind countenance, and his voice is inexpressibly sweet and persuasive. Those who came to scoff soon begin to listen. The minister draws a ghastly picture of the wretched career of a fallen woman. He points out how soon the pleasures of sin are over, and how terrible is the sequel. The girls do not appear very much affected, though they are subdued. Then the minister suddenly changes the current of his discourse. He awakens in the minds of those who listen to him the remembrance of their early days. He speaks of the home of childhood—he speaks of father and of mother. There is not a defiant countenance now. Tears are trickling down the cheeks of many. Some are on their knees, sobbing bitterly, and a few, a very few, leave the room. The guilty conscience can often resist an appeal to the terrors of the law; but to an appeal to nature, to goodness, and to the mercy and love of God, resistance is impossible. The minister proceeds in a voice half hushed with emotion, though still sweetly sounding, and asks the unfortunate ones why they do not return to the paths of peace and virtue. Are their parents still living? Then for their sakes he exhorts them to repentance. Are their parents dead? Then he exhorts them, by their memory, to repentance. Some persons suppose that the spirits of the dead hover over those they love. My sister, is your mother yet watching over you? Does she follow you from haunt to haunt of vice? Can you bear that thought? Is your mother yet watching over you—watching to see whether you will or will not forsake your career of misery, and be happy now and for ever? You don't forget your mother, my sister. Think of her. How she used to fondle you when you were a little child! Don't you remember how proud she was of you, and how, out of her little means, she dressed you in fine smart clothes? She was cross sometimes, and you were troublesome. Do you remember when you had had a quarrel how she came to your bedside? You pretended to be asleep, and she thought you were asleep, and shading the flaring candle with her hand, she bent over you and kissed you, and as she kissed you a tear fell upon your cheek. Remember those things now, my sister. Remember the day when you had to go to your first situation. How sorrowful your mother was while she was packing your trunk! What a large cake she put. into it, for fear you should be hungry! How carefully she put the bran-new Bible into it that father bought for you! You cannot forget the parting moment. You cannot forget how your father—he was a rough, hardworking man—how your father blessed his girl with a husky voice, and how he went out of the cottage suddenly and without waiting to see you off! You cannot forget how your mother, who had borne up so well, cried like a little child when she said "Good-bye," and how she bade you be an honest girl and not to forget God. Do you remember how your young brother told you he would be a man soon, and that he would get money, and you should not have to go to service? Your little sissy told you to send her a fine doll from London. Then the neighbour, who had come to carry your trunk to the station, took it up and left the cottage, and you followed him. As you passed through the little garden—how neatly father kept it!—the dog—a big ugly dog—came bounding against you, and you stooped down and suffered it to lick your face! It was a weary journey, though not quite a mile to the station. You did not pass a house or a tree, or a hedge, that did not recall some scene of the past. Do you remember how you kept up your spirits by the hope of returning to that dear home? Are they all dead, my sister? If not, go to those who have loved you, and who love you still. It may be father and mother are dead. Dead, yet living for ever. Living now, and watching to see if to-night you will accept the offer of mercy and of happiness. What answer will you make? Surely, surely, you will not for ever and ever be parted from them. Surely, surely, you will not spurn them. Surely, surely, you will not spurn the love and mercy of our Saviour.

When the minister ceased, he and the other gentlemen left the platform, and went to the girls and sat beside them. The minister placed himself by one who was leaning over the table with her face buried in her hands. The minister spoke to her, and she said, sullenly, " Leave me alone. I wish I had never come here." But the minister was not to be so repulsed. He put his hand upon her arm, and said, " Come, my dear, speak to me, and tell me how old you are." The girl looked up, and angrily replied, " I am sixteen." Only sixteen! What a wan face! A face not furrowed by Time, in preparation for the harvest of Eternity, but distorted by care and dissipation. " I have a daughter about your age," replied the minister, " and I pray you talk with me." It was a hard battle between good and evil. " It is no use talking," said the girl, " I don't want to be good. I only want to die, and be let alone. Everybody despises me and hates me, and I hate everybody. Do let me alone." The minister persevered. He drew the girl close to him and talked to her about his daughter, and he talked so hopefully, so lovingly, that at length the girl was overcome, and she told him some particulars of her life. The same old story. The same story of deception and ruin that almost all the unfortunates have to tell. The minister asked her if her father yet lived. No, he was dead. Her mother? Dead. "Come, my child," said the minister, "let me be your father." He pleaded with that girl as though he was pleading for his own life. Still the battle was not yet won. She would not go to a "home" then, but she would think about it. That would not do for the minister. He wanted her then and there to begin a life of virtue. She was his child; he could not suffer her even for a night to be in a place of infamy. At last, at the eleventh hour, there was joy in heaven over a repentant sinner. The minister took the girl to a refuge, and she was not the first by many whom he had rescued.

IN A LONDON POLICE COURT.

WITHIN a sixpenny cab fare of Regent Street, near to the mansions of the rich, within a stone's throw of one of the finest churches in the metropolis, but situated in a narrow lane, where squalor and misery reign supreme, is the police court to which we paid a visit at about noon.

We cannot say that

> Such a sight as we saw there,
> No mortal saw before,

but we do not want to repeat the visit. Not that we saw anything exceptional. It was a commonplace drama, which is daily enacted in each of the London police courts.

The court is small, and has not the slightest pretensions to architectural beauty. It is as plain and inconvenient as a third-class railway carriage. The magistrate, a benevolent-looking, elderly gentleman, was perched upon a raised platform, seated in an uncomfortable-looking easy chair, and before him was a small table, having on it one or two dirty-looking law books. Just below him, and before another small table, covered with papers, sat a sharp-looking individual, the clerk of the court. There were two attorneys seated at a third table. One of them was dressed in the height of " gentism;" the other had evidently been running to seed for the last three or four years, and from the hue of his shirt, and the absence of collar, we inferred that he had a difficulty with his laundress, who had most inconsiderately and inconveniently laid a *distringas* on his limited stock of long cloth and linen. Between these professionals sat the public press, represented by a bald-headed, blue-nosed, shabby personage, who had "flimsied" the proceedings of the court for at least a quarter of a century. Next to the witness-box stood the usher, whose business it was to call silence every twenty-two-and-a-half seconds, and to administer the usual oath in an unusually flippant manner. A few policemen, shrouded in the inimitable ugliness of their uniform, intensified the dismal appearance of things in general. The British public was represented by from thirty to forty persons of both sexes. The most conscientious dealer in old garments would not have given £5 for all the clothes they had on. A few came out of curiosity; old men with unshaven chins, who were continually snuffling, or blowing their ancient noses on large silk-patterned cotton pocket handkerchiefs. We were informed that these ancients came day after day, and year after year, but where they came from, or where they went to, no one knew, or cared to know. Most of the visitors were present to look after their friends who were in durance vile, and to learn their fate. As we are describing an English court of justice, it is superfluous to add that the place was badly ventilated, and the subordinate officers ill-mannered.

The night charges were being proceeded with when we entered. Out of these, at least ninety per cent. were charges of drunkenness, or of offences directly resulting from drunkenness. Although we regard drunkenness as a great social evil, we were pleased that the magistrate treated these cases with considerable leniency. With such miserable homes as poor townspeople have, no wonder that they flock to the gaily-lighted, and, to them, palatial public-houses. We were speculating on what became of those who could not pay the small fines, when a gentleman who occupied a seat next to us, and appeared to know everything and everybody, informed us that if they could not pay, they were dismissed in the afternoon, on the arrival of the van. We were glad to think that so many escaped a ride in those horrid looking police vans—gloomy, funeral hearses, in which the morally dead are carried to prison; and in which sometimes, unhappily, judgment erring, the morally living are unhearsed with the morally dead.

A young girl was brought before the magistrate. Her accuser was a policeman; her crime, singing and shouting in a respectable street after twelve o'clock at night. She was not known to the officers of the court. She said it was the first time she had ever been in custody. These were the only words she spoke, and we believe them. She was about eighteen. Her finely formed face would have been called classic and angelic if she had been rich. But she was only a poor work girl. No wonder—though a thousand pities—that she sought pleasure in the only way she could find it. Plying her needle from morning to night, when night came she needed excitement more than rest. So with some companions she sang and made a noise in a respectable street.

The magistrate addressed her kindly. While he was speaking, the girl turned round and looked at us. A fearful daring glance—a glance that said, "Here, look into my heart, I do not care how bad you think me. I have been in prison. I care not for any one's opinion—I care not how bad I become."

She was dismissed, and as she left the court with her friends she coloured and smiled—almost laughed. Poor creature! her night's recreation will be to her the beginning of greater sorrows than she has dreamed of. Let not the gaol bird any more pretend to virtue, especially amongst her companions and neighbours. That one night's incarceration will rid her of the last vestige of self-respect, and the Tempter will find her an easy prey.

Of course such creatures must not make a noise in respectable streets at midnight. It is intolerable that young ladies just returned from the opera, and retired to their downy beds, should be disturbed by the noise of a person who was only created to make ball-dresses and opera cloaks. Be it so. Let it be granted that the policeman must drag them to the station-house. Is that not sufficient punishment? Could not the case be disposed of privately? By all means let there be no noise in respectable streets at midnight, unless it proceed from respectable houses; but, if possible, let us devise some means of keeping silence without bringing poor girls to shame.

Whilst the magistrate was disposing of the case of a man who had endeavoured to cheat one of those social innocents—those extremely benevolent creatures, called pawnbrokers—there was a hubbub and screaming outside the court, and, as soon as the naughty man who had tried to cheat the good, confiding "three balls," had been remanded for a week, two females were rudely pushed into the dock. They were mother and daughter; the latter a child about ten years of age, the former had seen, perhaps, forty summers. They were both thin and famished-looking. They were both clad in rags. They were both panting; they seemed to us like creatures who were being hunted to their death. They glanced at the witness-box, at their pursuer, and accuser. There he stood, in some respects the most repulsive looking mortal we ever set eyes upon—fat, sleek, and well dressed. We could not help making a mental calculation as to the quantity of tallow that might have been obtained by boiling him down. His dark hair showed the extreme oiliness of his nature. A soft, puffy, doughy hand—a hand that could not know what it was to give an honest, friendly grasp. His face pleased us best, for it was a deep red—red even to the tips of the ears and to the fat throat. This redness pleased us, for it seemed like an unwilling flush of shame—like a signal set up by nature to warn us of danger, and bid us beware of the man. His eyes—well, we cannot say much about them. They were always cast down, as if seeking for some brother reptile. When he was sworn, he kissed the book with a smack. We were sorry the worthy magistrate did not ask him if he knew the nature of an oath.

Then he commenced his accusation with his eyes still seeking for a brother reptile. He said he was an officer of some society, and also a constable. His business appeared to consist in preventing anything like an appearance of poverty in respectable streets—his business was to hunt beggars to their holes, and, if possible, keep them there till they were starved. With regard to the mother and daughter present, he had suspected them from their appearance, had stealthily watched them, and at last had seen them coming up or going down some area steps with a basket in their hands. He took them into custody, they resisted, and the daughter kicked his legs.

Capital! Did she hurt them much? Why were they not exhibited in open court?

Then, hysterical and crying, the woman gave the lie to all this sleek, reptile-hunting witness had said. She had not been down the area; she was not dishonest. Her basket only contained (and she produced it) a few combs that she had for sale. Her husband used to be a good man, but now he was a drunkard and a wife-beater, and she bared her arms—that is, she put aside her ragged shawl, and showed them covered with bruises. She knew no other way of getting a living for herself and child. That man (she pointed to the sleek, reptile-hunting witness) had a spite against her—he followed her everywhere.

Much more in the torrent of her sorrow, her vehement hysterical passion, and, as we believe, of her innocency, did she pour forth. The scalding tears fell from the mother's eyes. The daughter looked too terrified even to weep. Her eyes were fixed upon her sleek, reptile-hunting accuser, fascinated, as it were by her terror, as though she gazed upon a serpent.

The officers of the court knew nothing against her, and, good fellows, they responded to the appeal of the magistrate as though they were disgusted with the sleek accuser. In her basket there was nothing but a few combs and kettle-holders, and in her pockets twopence halfpenny, a crust of bread, and some bits of meat she had picked up on a step. It was clear that she had not been robbing. Then, why in the name of justice, was she not dismissed? A well-dressed person would not be detained in custody for an instant on a mere suspicion, and why should there be a distinction between rags and a good coat? It seems, however, that it is a criminal offence for a poor person to come near a rich man's habitation. Your modern Lazarus is sent to prison if he sits at the gate of your modern Dives. The sleek, reptile-seeking accuser swore he saw her go down an area and come up again. She declared it was false. Despite his good coat and her rags, we believe her.

The woman was remanded to make inquiries. And the sleek accuser wriggled out of court.

The night charges were ended. The first remanded case was that of a young man charged with forgery. But we had seen enough for one day, and we left. What became of the dismissed girl; what was the fate of the remanded vendor of combs and kettle-holders and her daughter, we know not. We heartily wish that our property might be entrusted to the guardianship of the police only, and that Society officers in plain clothes were not permitted to hunt the poor like bloodhounds.

LIFE IN BARRACKS.

———o———

It may be that the world will grow wise before it grows good, and that even whilst men still learn the art of war, and long before the lion lies down with the lamb, there will be an end to standing armies. Of course, seeing that unregenerate human nature is what it is, an armed police is necessary in most countries. But what we mean by standing armies are those enormous establishments that are kept up in times of peace against times of war. These prevent us paying off our war debts when we are at peace. Putting aside China and all other barbarous, and savage, and semi-savage countries, the world owes for war debts not less than three thousand millions of pounds sterling. Whenever we see pauperism, or vice, the accursed fruit of pauperism, we always think how the devil must chuckle over the invention of standing armies. We do not assume that the doing away with standing armies would make wars to cease, though it would make them less frequent. But this is the point. A soldier of three months' standing is, after a month in the field, just as good a veteran as the soldier of ten years' standing. In these days, when electric telegraphy, by keeping us well informed about our neighbours, makes a surprise impossible, there is no reason why there should be a standing army, except for the purpose of internal police.

Halt! Here we are, like the Rev. Pat O'Connor, of Cork, spluttering out the morality in the wrong place. The Rev. Pat always prepared a grand bit of morality for the end of his sermons, but he was so anxious to give it forth, that he read his sermons backwards—that is, he began with the morality and finished with the text. It was our intention to wind up with a hint about standing armies, but it would come out first. There is this consolation for the reader, that he is to be bothered with no more of the moralities.

Did you ever go to barracks? Did you ever pass an hour in a canteen? We have done so, and we propose to give an outline of the manner in which our standing army kills time when it is lying idle, which, having read, you will forgive our preliminary moralisations.

We selected for our purpose a small barracks near to London, at which is stationed a detachment of a cavalry regiment. We made this selection because we knew a chum of the sergeant-major, the non-commissioned officer who has charge of the discipline, morals, and horses of the said detachment.

At the barracks we were introduced to the sergeant-major —commonly called "the major." A finer specimen of the genus British soldier it would be hard to find. About 5ft. 10½in. in height, robust limbs, a bronze complexion, and, with his accoutrements, riding twenty-two stone—not bearded like the pard, and only moderately supplied with familiar oaths. The major was in the Indian mutiny and the Crimea, and has plenty of decorations. It was non-commissioned officers like the major who won the battle of Inkerman, and who are on all occasions the back-bone of the army. It is men like the major who utilise the pluck and dash of epauletted striplings from Eton and from Harrow.

Having liquored, we visited the stables. Cleaner and better appointed stables are neither desirable nor possible. The horses were perfectly groomed and in beautiful condition; their coats were as shiny as the metal on the harness which was hanging up before each stall. Some of the animals were finer than others, but all were excellent. The average cost is £25, and the like horses would cost a private gentleman at least £100. To be sure, cavalry horses have the best chance of doing well and looking well. Plenty to eat, any quantity of grooming, and very little work, agree admirably with the equine species. It will be a happy day for England when her peasantry and the poor in her towns are as comfortably lodged and as well fed as the British cavalry horses. A ragged, starving urchin, seeing a lady's lapdog gently carried in the arms of a flunkey, exclaimed, "My eyes, don't I wish father were a dog, and I were a pup like that there!" If the peasantry—say of Dorsetshire—could have a glimpse of the stables of the British cavalry horses, how they would envy the sleek quadrupeds! God knows, that so far as mundane happiness is concerned, they have cause for such envy. This is not moralising; it is a huge fact that we cannot pass by without a word of comment. No one who has visited the hovel homes of England and then stood in a barrack stable can avoid the reflection that it is happier, so far as the flesh is concerned, to be a British cavalry horse than a British peasant.

Having spent a short time with the horses, we ascended to the part of the building occupied by the men. On the way we met the commanding officer, a young captain—a Bond-street dandy, with fluff upon his youthful lip, but who would play the hero in the fray. He was smoking a cigar, and his countenance betrayed an inward conviction that he was, by the decree of Providence, monarch of more than any mortal eye, aided by the most powerful telescope, could survey. It was our privilege to hear him address a few words to the major, and if there had been any previous doubt in our mind as to the blueness of his blood, it would have been removed by the "y" twang that distinguishes the pronunciation of the young British swell. We find no fault with the gallant captain. It does not require a development of brain to render a man first-rate food for powder.

The quarters of the soldiers are as clean as whitewash can make them. Eight men sleep in one room. The iron bedsteads were turned up, and the bedding was neatly folded, strapped, and laid upon them. In one corner of the room were the carbines and the swords. At a table in the middle of the room were four soldiers in undress—that is, in their shirt sleeves—at dinner. Each man had a portion of beef and potatoes in a white basin, and so far as we could perceive, there was no reason to grumble at the rations. One of the diners remarked to a comrade that the beef was " awfully more-ish," which the major told us was the common complaint, but added, " If they was to get a joint a-piece, they would call out for more."

For the inspection of the men's quarters the major had put us under the charge of a corporal, and this person gave us a little insight into barrack existence. The men are partially employed till, say, half-past twelve o'clock. They have to saddle their horses, and to go out for exercise at nine. At half-past eleven they have to parade, on parade days. They return to barracks, and brush up their accoutrements and pipeclay their gloves, their trouser-stripes, and the white patches in their uniform. This pipe-claying is a tedious process in the winter, as it requires heat, and the supply of coals is strictly limited. After 1 P.M.—at the latest—the work of the day is over in barracks. The soldiers go to canteen, or to visit friends, and, if they require it, can always obtain a pass till twelve o'clock at night. As these passes are given without any inquiry, we cannot understand why the leave is not fixed at midnight, which would save the commanding officer the trouble of signing a lot of papers. It may be, however, that the object is to give the commanding officers something to do. How soldiers on leave employ their time is well known: either they are at the public-house or else paying temporary addresses to the housemaids and cooks. The corporal informed us that the private gets 8d. a day clear. Now there cannot be much dissipation upon 8d. a day, but soldiers have other sources of income. Their friends frequently send them money, all of which is needed for pleasure only. The corporal, who is an intelligent man, said that, taking the rich with the poor, the private did not spend less than 10s. a week. We expect from the flourishing circumstances of the canteen keeper, who, by-the-way, does not get all the soldier's custom, that the corporal's average is below rather than above the actual amount.

From the barracks, once more under the escort of the major, we went to the canteen. There is nothing attractive either in the exterior or interior of the place. The poorest beer-shop in a fourth-rate provincial town is superior to it as to architecture and accommodation. It is a long, low, dismal-looking building. Turning off sharp to the right is the bar, and behind that is what is called by courtesy a parlour. The canteen is the major's head-quarters; at least, he considers it his duty to visit it not less than six times a day, and to be the last to leave at night. Round the bar fire, in a little recess, are some seats for the accommodation of the landlord, landlady, the major, and the major's friends. We were politely called within the bar, and accommodated with pipes, tobacco, spittoons, and beer. Spirits are not allowed to be sold in the canteen, and consequently the men are obliged to go to the public-houses if they want grog. This seems to us a senseless regulation. If the soldiers want spirits they get them outside the barracks. Why then should they not have them in the canteen, where they would be purer and cheaper? The canteen prices are regulated by authority, and the goods sold are of excellent quality. Any well-founded complaints would put the canteen-keeper's profitable monopoly in jeopardy.

Round the bar-room was ranged a number of cans and pots, enough for the accommodation, one would suppose, of a regiment. On a small counter was bacon, cheese, saveloys, tea, coffee, tobacco, and needles and thread. On a shelf beneath the counter we noticed bread and soap, butter and blacking, in uninviting confusion. The canteen-keeper is bound to supply all the requirements of the soldier, even to the means of sewing on his buttons and stitching up the

rents in his clothes. The landlady is as much unlike the
ordinary landlady as one can well conceive. She is a thin,
spare body, with a sharp eye for business; and in her line
a sharp eye and an equable temper are indispensable. She
treated the sergeant-major with deference, and laughed at
his jokes; but the privates were dealt with in an off-hand
business manner. The dame was rather out of humour with
the authorities. The barracks had just lost a detachment
in consequence, it was said, of some irregularities. She
declared it was all stuff, and that a steadier set of men never
trod in shoe-leather. "Indeed," she remarked, "they are
too steady for business; for one can't get one's salt out of
their custom."

We bow to her experience, or otherwise we should not
have supposed that the men were too steady. The demands
for beer and tobacco were incessant, and a horrible hubbub
of loud talking, mingled with profane swearing, came
through the partition which separated the tap-room from
the parlour. Perhaps there was more noise than usual, for
the landlord remarked that "the boys were going the whole
hog." The major invited us to a game of cards. He
thought cribbage the best game on the cards, but he was
not particular. He could play "put," or all-fours, or whist.
We declined cards, preferring to listen to his Crimean and
Indian experiences. Having done so, and drunk much beer
to the detriment of our stomach, and smoked with vigour
for upwards of an hour, we took our departure from the
canteen.

Rather a bald sketch this! That is not our fault. We
set down only what we see and hear, and life in barracks is
a bald blank life. It is a sort of stunted, festering vegeta-
tion. What there is in it may be noted down on a single
leaf of a small pocket-book. The soldier in barracks is
not employed for more than four hours per day. What he
does out of barracks does not now concern us. All he does
in barracks is to look after his accoutrements, to eat, to sleep,
to drink, to swear, to smoke, to tell nasty stories, and to

sing nasty songs. We are not censuring the soldier. Crowd a lot of men together and let them be idle nearly all day, and moral deterioration is inevitable. Considering the life of soldiers in barracks, we marvel that they are as they are, and we ought to be thankful that they are not infinitely worse than they are.

A BEGGARS' SUPPER AND A THIEVES' HOP.

———o———

WITHIN a mile of the Bank of England stands the celebrated Aldgate Pump, and fifty yards beyond that is Aldgate Church. This spot may be fitly described as the confluence of the many and diverse streams of London life. At this point four roads meet. That to the west, which at Aldgate Pump is subdivided, leads through the main arteries of the City—every yard of ground worth a prince's ransom —to the political and fashionable West-end. The road to the north takes us through the Hebrew quarter to Bishopsgate Street, and from thence we can proceed to any of those northern suburbs that are inhabited by what stump-orators call the great middle class. The southernly road is to the Thames *via* the London and St. Catherine's Docks. The road due east is called Whitechapel, and it is no affectation to say that the inhabitants of Whitechapel differ from the rest of the London community as much as though three thousand miles of ocean instead of thirty yards of paving-stones separated them from the rich City, the aristocratic West-end, the respectable suburbanites of the north, and the thriving and amphibious creatures who prowl about the docks and wharves. At nine o'clock in the evening of a sultry summer's day we found ourselves in this peculiar locality for the purpose of keeping an appointment. We were a little too soon, and our acquaintance was a little behind time; consequently we had an opportunity of looking at the place and people. The passers-by were a dirty crowd, with a small sprinkling of rather clean persons. Never before have we seen such a number of ragged children and squalid women. The children were of small stature, and their faces were wan and so old that the little ones might have passed muster for adult dwarfs. Many of the women were without bonnets, and it was plain enough that they did their part towards supporting the numerous gin-palaces that abound in Whitechapel. We noticed as a peculiarity, that though it was a summer's night—the thermometer about 75—a majority of the men wore great coats. A few negroes, probably marine cooks, and several German sugar-bakers were loafing about. Of course there were respectably-clad people, and these were proceeding eastward to their homes at Mile-end and Bow. Several "traps," that is, vehicles above a tradesman's cart and below a gentleman's carriage, were also passing eastward, taking their owners to Epping and other dismal villages on the borders of the dreariest and dampest forest in England. The spot selected for our meeting was the Aldgate end of Butcher's Row. A veritable row of butchers' shambles. Business was over for the night; but there were the red-stained blocks, and the strong smell of uncooked meat. We were beginning to find fault with our folly in supposing that our acquaintance would keep his promise, when up he came with an apology for being late. We assured the Rev. Joseph Wilkinson, D.D., that we fully excused his want of punctuality.

The Rev. Joseph Wilkinson was a striking specimen of faded clerical gentility. He had on a paletot, and one marvelled how a garment could be so threadbare and yet free from holes. His hat—half-covered with a cloth hatband—was napless, but scrupulously brushed. His white choker was tolerably clean, but tumbled, like the white chokers of waiters and undertakers. His clerical waistcoat, buttoning up to the chin, was a shiny black. His trousers were also shiny, particularly about the knees, and rather ragged about the heels. Now, whether Mr. Wilkinson was ever ordained we know not. Our impression is that he had not been ordained, and that he had no title to write D.D. after his name. Three weeks before the meeting now referred to

Mr. Wilkinson had introduced himself to us, presenting a letter from a highly-esteemed friend, and also showing us letters from Church dignitaries. The object of the visit was to ask for a small subscription towards building a church in a fishing village on the coast of Cornwall. Mr. Wilkinson gave us a pathetic description of the spiritual destitution of the village. There was no church and no minister. His own means were utterly exhausted, and unless he obtained help he must give up—his eyes were suffused with tears when he said this—he must give up the work of evangelisation. The poor people got their livelihood by catching pilchards, and he trusted that the community which they helped to feed would not allow their immortal souls to perish. We were not to be done. We thought from the first that the Rev. Joseph Wilkinson, D.D., was a swindler, and we were right. In less than eight-and-forty hours, by the aid of a clever detective, we hunted our man down, and found him to be one of the most notorious begging-letter impostors in the metropolis. We had another interview with Mr. Wilkinson, and he begged hard that we would not prosecute, which, as we had not been victimised, we had no intention of doing. So far from that, we gave Mr. Wilkinson a cigar and a glass of grog, and he was so obliging as to give us a little insight into the art and mystery of professional begging.

"There, my dear sir," said Mr. Wilkinson, examining the spoon with which he was stirring his grog, to see if it was Hall-marked, "a man may beg on the square and he is safe from the law, but if he is a little ingenious, if he exercises intellect, he is liable to punishment. I am in jeopardy, not that I do more harm than a common street beggar, but because I have the instincts of a gentleman, and I cannot adopt a vulgar calling."

The philosophical vagabond, after another glass of grog, invited us to accompany him one evening to sup with some beggars who had formed a club, and met together once or twice a week. Mr. Wilkinson offered to call for us, but for two reasons we declined giving him that trouble. We did not like to incur the risk of diminishing our limited stock of plate, and we rather shrank from walking through the streets with a notorious impostor. Hence we fixed upon Whitechapel, in which neighbourhood the supper party assembled, as the rendezvous.

Mr. Wilkinson informed us that, warned by the risk he had encountered, he was now living on the " square." He had given up the begging-letter business and had gone into the coal trade. He was selling coals on commission, and was doing very well. Mr. Wilkinson might have spared his breath. We knew him, and we are not so soft as prison chaplains. We have given our servants strict orders to shut the door in the face of any person dressed as a clergyman who comes to solicit an order for coals. Mr. Wilkinson confessed he was rather hard-up. We were sorry for him. Could we put him in the way of doing a bit of "stiff"— that is an accommodation bill for £20? We could not assist him. Would we cash his I.O.U. for £5. We declined the precious autograph, but we lent him £2 without acknowledgment. Mr. Wilkinson assured us that his word was as good as his bond. No doubt about it; but what is his bond worth?

As the two sovereigns were dropped into Mr. Wilkinson's waistcoat pocket, we turned into the "Jolly Dogs," rather a shabby-looking public-house, at the corner of a blind court. A corpulent landlady was behind the bar, who seemed exhilarated at the advent of Mr. Wilkinson. "Why, parson!" she exclaimed, "we had almost guv' you up. The tripes is on the table." The parson blessed her in a most uncanonical manner, and ordered a glass of gin and bitters. The flacid eye of the corpulent landlady was fixed upon us. "What did we want?" The parson told her to mind her own business, and again bestowed upon her an uncanonical blessing. We went upstairs to the supper-room, and found the brethren already at work with their knives and forks. We were accommodated with a seat next to the chairman—a young man "out of business," of rather flashy appearance. We were afterwards informed that this gentleman, Charley Fluker, was well known to the police as a person who associated with men who did not thoroughly comprehend the difference between *meum* and *teum*. It was a tripe supper, and on the table was tripe dressed in various ways. There was tripe fried in onions and tripe fried in batter. There was tripe boiled in milk, and plain boiled tripe. There was stewed tripe, and tripe "toad-in-the-hole." The dish most in request was tripe boiled in milk. The consumption was wonderful. The "distressed tradesman," who said he could eat "a waistcoat of it," gobbled up, we should say, a yard of tripe, and probably on the average each guest ate about two pounds of tripe, seasoned with about half-an-ounce of mustard. We have frequently noticed the skill with which a cat laps up milk, but still more remarkable was the knack with which the beggars lapped up the gravy with their knives. It seemed to be a point of etiquette that under no circumstances should the fork be put to the mouth. Whilst the supper was proceeding there was no conversation; but it could hardly be said that any time was lost. In about fifteen minutes the guests had filled their capacious stomachs to repletion. Waistcoats were unbuttoned, the *debris* of the feast were cleared away, and the chairman got upon his legs.

"Now, my blokes," said he, "the gent to my right, who is our visitor, wishes you to take a glass with him. Order what you like, let it be hot and strong as blazes, and he will pay the shot."

The ten guests received this brief speech with applause, and the waiter was favoured with orders for gin and water and rum and water. Before executing them, the waiter, who was evidently of a suspicious temperament, came to us for the money. The "distressed tradesman" suggested that we should wet both eyes, and order two glasses of grog at once, to save trouble. To this we had no objection, and forthwith paid for twenty-two grogs, at sixpence per glass.

The first toast was, "Our noble selves;" the next was, "Our guest and all liberal souls." In proposing our health the "distressed tradesman" said:—"Christian friends and beloved brethren, I wish I could do justice to this toast. But like a dear relative of mine who died at the expense of the Government, though I am a 'willain' man, unfortunately like Cain I aint able. Our guest is a liberal soul and no flies. He has wetted both our eyes, and when that lot is sponged up, I'll bet a Dutch herring to a Peeler, and that, I take it, is about a hundred to one—(cheers)—that the liberal soul will order a third glass to wet our blowpipes. My Christian friends and brethren, we ought to honour the swell who raises spirits from the vasty deep—my spirits are often under my *soles*—by pouring spirits down. All the harm we wish him is, that he may be as happy and live as jolly as a beggar." After this toast the beggars indulged in harmony. About the songs, it will be sufficient to remark that the vocalisation was not unworthy of the words. Whilst the singing was going on, the chairman and the parson pointed out to us some of the leading beggars. There was the "distressed tradesman," a model of seedy respectability. His business was carried on in the suburbs. Accompanied by two respectably-dressed children, whom he hired at a shilling a day and their food, he walked about the streets bawling out, "Christian friends! A poor and unfortunate tradesman is forced to ask your charity to keep him and his dear children from starvation. After a long struggle with difficulties I was sold up by an unfeeling creditor, and with my family turned penniless upon the world. I hope, now, by your aid, my Christian friends, to be able to emigrate and begin a new life in Australia. Oh, my friends, I pray give me the smallest relief, and Heaven will bless your store." The parson observed that the "distressed tradesman" was a profitable but rather a hard line. The perpetual bawling in the streets was fatiguing. We remarked that the "distressed tradesman" looked very pale. The chairman rejoined that he would look more lively if he washed his face, and upon a closer inspection we found that he was made up for his *role* with paint.

The vendor of lucifer matches was rather an old man, in ragged garments. His little emag—emag is the flash word for game—was to beseech ladies to help him to get an honest livelihood by buying a box of matches. He sold very few lucifers, but he collected plenty of pence. Seated next to this person was a stalwart man dressed as a sailor, who devoted his energies to collecting money to take him down to Liverpool to join his ship. In marked contrast to the sailor was the old soldier, dressed in a faded and nondescript uniform. This individual went the round of the public-houses, and obtained money from those who believed his story that he had been unfairly treated by the authorities. There was present a very lugubrious looking beggar who sold tracts. His plan was to step up to likely-looking ladies, and ask them to direct him to the house of some clergyman or minister, and then to persuade them to buy a tract, which might be useful to the souls of their servants. There was also present a beggar with a stentorian voice, who sold and sang songs in the street. He frequented so-called quiet neighbourhoods, and generally planted himself before a house where some of the blinds were drawn down in token of sickness, and his ingenuity was often rewarded by small donations to go into another street.

We asked Charley Fluker whether professional begging paid. "Certainly," said that gentleman, "it is one of the best businesses out. No matter what line a man is in, he can easily do a hundred streets a-day; and he must be a muff if he cannot get a penny out of each street. These fellows, on the average, get twelve shillings a-day, and the best of them *earn* their pound."

We commend this fact to the benevolent public, who, in spite of the admonitions of the anti-Mendicity Society, persist in giving their alms to street beggars.

The two glasses of grog being exhausted, the "distressed tradesman" proposed another glass all round in honour of the guest, and he was good enough to remark "that we were a first-rate cove, and ought to be in their line." Mollified by this compliment, we could not resist the appeal to our purse for more grog.

Charley Fluker observed that it was rather slow work, and asked us if we would like to go to a hop in the neighbourhood, to which we assented. Before leaving the supper-room we had to shake hands with the brethren; but, foreseeing this, we had prudently encased our hand in a glove. Sooth to say, we were by no means fascinated with the brethren, and of the two we would rather shake hands with a burglar than with a professional beggar.

Under the escort of Charley, the parson declining to join us in the excursion, we went to an assembly room not far from where stands the Garrick Theatre. It was a low uncleanly room, and the atmosphere was almost stifling. It was, we believe, duly licensed for music and dancing. The music consisted of a fiddle and wind instruments, and the dancing was a species of rough indecent romping. Charley told us to take care of our watch, as the place was a resort of thieves. The women were of the worst and vilest class. It was a scene of vice in all its naked deformity. There were several seamen who were doomed to be drugged and plundered by their partners. The keeper of this saloon, with a keen eye to profit, set one or two women to ask us to stand some wine. Charley told him and them to go to a certain warm place; but surely, if a life of vice is a passport to that warm place, the admonition was needless. "You must stand some sherry," said Charley, "but don't drink it." Accordingly we ordered two bottles of sherry, at the moderate price of 8s. 6d. per bottle. The considerate Charley introduced us to a man whose flattened nose showed that he was practically acquainted with the noble art of self-defence, and we soon found the advantage of the introduction. There was a clamorous demand for more wine, with sundry threats and pushes, but our pugilistic acquaintance was a very efficient guard, and quickly restored order as far as we were concerned. We were about to leave when there was a cry of "a ring! a ring!" and in the middle of the room were two women nearly stripped to their waists fighting. A more savage and inhuman spectacle cannot be conceived. Goaded on by the men, they were tearing each other's hair, striking each other on the breast, and with the cheap rings on their fingers were cutting each other's faces until they were covered with blood. In vain the keeper of the saloon called upon them to stop. They kept tearing at each other, now striking blows with their fists, and then, by way of variety, lacerating each other with their nails. We had recourse to our pugilistic acquaintance. We offered him a crown to stop the affair, and he accepted the offer. Not heeding the shouts and imprecations of the men who were looking on, he broke through the ring and dragged out one of the women. Charley suggested that we had better cut, and we were not loth to turn our back upon the most coarse and revolting orgies that can be witnessed in any capital in the world. We scarcely know which is the more disgusting—the Beggars' Supper or the Thieves' Hop. Both were singularly dull and nasty entertainments. It is the fashion of those who write tales of crime for the corruption of boys to invest their heroes with a certain air of romance. Our readers may gather from this sketch how thoroughly false are such descriptions of the lives of the criminal class.

FOUND DEAD.

Mr. TRIMMER was neither rogue nor fool. He was on the right side of the very finely drawn line that separates honesty from dishonesty, and being a fussy well-to-do individual, he was quite the bull's-eye of his own particular circle. Mr. Trimmer was not educated. Although an enterprising person, and combining the business of a milk walk with the vendition of greens and other vegetable matter fit for the human stomach, science had not taught his soul to wander so far as that flood of celestial glory which astronomers call the "milky way." Still Mr. Trimmer was a shrewd and smart fellow. He was chairman of a benefit society, and was even spoken of for the vestry. Yet Mr. Trimmer, though by no means addicted to humbling confessions frankly admitted that he was " floored." " There is more in this here than what meets the eye," said Mr. Trimmer, " and if I knows a carrot from a *mangle-vursal* there has been foul play. Don't tell me. Paupers ain't the sort to go a turning themselves into a hicicle for nothing nohow. It ain't their game. The *werdict* is given, but I am dumfoundered if I knows, or any other chap, what the case means."

The evidence was certainly very meagre. A woman (quite a chit of a gal and a hangel to look at, deposed Mrs. Dry), who represented her husband to be a traveller, took a room in the house of Mrs. Dry, in the New Cut. She was dull, and often cried, but did not seem to want for money. Her husband came to see her once, and a day or two after that she was confined. "A finer baby I never seed," deposed Mrs. Dry. A fortnight later there came a letter which quite upset the poor creature. The same night "(leastways it was nigh morning," deposed Mrs. Dry) there was an awful screaming, and when Mrs. Dry went into the lodger's room she found the baby was dead. The doctor certified that the mother had overlaid the child. The young creature took on badly, and had milk fever. In her delirium she talked about home and father and mother, and all those kind of things. When she got better she would not speak to anyone, but went out every day and came home at night nearly tired to death. On one occasion Mrs. Dry followed her, and the young woman walked to the City and strolled about up one street and down another in a strange sort of manner. Another letter came for the young woman, and that day she did not go out till late, and again Mrs. Dry followed her. In the City the young woman met the man who had called upon her—her husband—and they got into a cab and drove off. Mrs. Dry heard nothing more of her lodger until the police called on her and told her she was wanted to give evidence about a young woman who was found dead in the Park.

This was the sum total of the evidence, and therefore the mental fogginess of Mr. Trimmer is quite excusable. Suppose we try to clothe the skeleton with flesh, after the manner of the philosophers, who, from a few fossil remains give us pictures of the animals that lived upon the earth in pre-Adamite ages. We may not accurately solve the mystery that puzzles Mr. Trimmer, but we will write nothing that is not true to life. Alas! that such things are so true and so commom!

It was a November afternoon. Through the slush and dirt which abounds in the transpontine half of the metropolis, a cab, with a plain deal box on the roof, and a man and woman inside, drove until it reached a by-street in the New Cut, when the check-string admonished the driver to stop. Both the passengers were young. The man, rather good-looking and well dressed, was smoking a cigar, and was evidently out of temper. The woman was young and pretty, and appeared very nervous.

"Oh William," she said, "I wish you would go with me."

"Don't be a fool Mimmie," replied William, testily, "I don't want to be mixed up in this deuced affair. Go and get the lodging by yourself. I will wait here for you."

Mimmie got out of the cab, walked up the street, and knocked at Mrs. Dry's door. The door was open, and therefore the knocking produced, at least so thought Mimmie, a dreadful noise. Mrs. Dry, who was in the midst of her week's wash, came forward. Mimmie told her she wanted a room, and she was asked upstairs, and shown into the first floor front, a bedroom better furnished than might have been supposed from the outside of the premises. Mimmie said that her husband was a traveller, and he would not, at least for some time, be with her. Mrs. Dry coughed knowingly, and remarked that it made no difference. Then as to terms. Usually the room let for six shillings a week, but under certain circumstances — Mrs. Dry glanced at Mimmie's figure—the rent was higher. No matter, what would the rent be?

"Say ten shillings a week," replied Mrs. Dry: "that is if you can afford it, my dear. But lor, don't tremble so."

Mrs. Dry was a rough but a kind woman. She had her weaknesses. She was fond of a little gossip, she was prone to indulge in stimulants, and she was apt to let kind feelings interfere with business. She—to quote her own expression—took to Mimmie from the first, and would have taken her in at any price. Mrs. Dry told Mimmie it was nothing to go through after all. She was the mother of six, and ought to know. She would do the nursing, and there was not a cleverer doctor in the world than Mr. Simpkin, in the Cut, and he only charged ten shillings. So it was all arranged, and having paid a week in advance—Mrs. Dry did not ask for it—Mimmie left, promising to return shortly.

William rated her for being such a confounded time, but he was mollified when he heard that the business had been settled, without giving him any further trouble.

"William dear," said the girl, "it almost breaks my heart to leave you. Come and see me often, it will be so dull."

"You won't see much of me just now, and so don't think it, Mimmie. And you won't see me at all if you go on blubbering like that, for I hate crying women."

Mimmie tried to smile. William paid the cabman, and told him where to drive to.

"Good bye," said William, holding out his hand, "I must be off."

"Don't leave me without a kiss," said Mimmie.

"Don't make yourself a fool in the streets," rejoined William. However he put his head into the cab and kissed her, and Mimmie went to Mrs. Dry's.

A sorrowful time of it had poor Mimmie. Nothing to do but to brood upon the past, and afraid to speculate upon the future. She could not, would not, think that he could mean to be unkind, yet he did not come to her or even write to her. He was no doubt too busy, and it was insolent of that woman, Mrs. Dry, to ask her if her husband was kind. The doctor saw her, and told her that she must walk every day, but she would not leave the room. What, go out, and perhaps William might call! So she sat by the window, watching from morning until night. Sometimes she would open the window, and look up and down the street, but she looked in vain. At length, however, William came, and greeted her with a chiding for writing to him.

"I suppose that you want to get me into a mess; but I won't stand it. You must just keep quiet until the affair is over."

"You will come to me then, William dear. Oh, darling, you will come then and see me and our—our little one."

"Yes, but don't bother," said William, "I am going from town for a week or two, and so just keep quiet."

"Must you go now, William? I am so frightened, dear. I think I shall die if you are far away."

"Stuff about dying," said William, "you will be all right."

Mimmie sat herself on his knee, and for a few minutes

William spoke to her and kissed her as in days of yore, and the sad heart once again beat with joy. That night Mimmie slept—next morning she talked cheerfully to Mrs. Dry.

A fortnight passes. Mimmie is in bed, and lying by her is the baby. "He said for two weeks," murmured Mimmie, "and perhaps he will be here to night" And she drew the baby to her and kissed it. "Your father will see you soon," she said, "and I know he will love you." Mrs. Dry brought her a letter. "Quick, bring a light, good nurse; I know it is to tell me he is coming."

Mrs. Dry stood by the bedside holding a candle. Trembling with eagerness Mimmie opened the letter. It was as follows:—

Dear Mimmie,—I have ascertained that you are well, and I am glad of it. I think it is better for both our sakes that I should tell you the truth. It is no use our meeting again. It will bring you and me to ruin. I will provide for the child, but I will not see it. This will not give you more pain to read than it does me to write; but if you really love me, you will see it is for the best. I enclose you a bank note to go on with, and in a week or two I will make final arrangements through a friend. If you don't make any fuss or bother it will be best for both of us. You can put the child out, and no one need know it is yours. I hope, dear Mimmie, you will marry a better husband than I could have made you, and become a respectable woman. I shall always think of you with affection, particularly if you fall in with my views. Good bye.

WILLIAM.

She read it again and again. "Hold the light nearer," she said, "I can't see." She read it again. "Oh God, what shall I do?" Mrs. Dry put down the candle and said, "Is it bad news, dear; is he ill?" Mimmie made a great and successful effort to conceal her poignant sorrow. "It is nothing, nursey; it is nothing, nursey, and I will tell you of it to morrow." Then she lay down and pretended to sleep. Mrs. Dry said she would sit up with her, but Mimmie would not allow her.

She slept for a short time, if mere dreamy unconsciousness is sleep. When she awoke she muttered, "It can't be so, my eyes have deceived me, I will read it again." She got out of bed, but was too weak to stand. So she slid upon the floor, and slowly and painfully wriggled herself to the corner of the room where the dim night-light was burning. She read the letter again, and there was no longer room for doubt. Back she wriggled herself in the same way to the bedside, but had no power to raise herself. After a while, she got upon her knees, and so remained, repeating over and over again, "God have mercy upon me!" The child cried. This roused her to fresh exertions. She got upon the bed, she took the child in her arms, and she fell upon it fainting.

Two hours at least, she remained in a state of unconsciousness. When she came to herself her first thought was the child. She half raised herself on the pillows and looked at it. It was warm, but it was dead. It did not occur to her at first that it was dead, and she thought it was asleep. Yet it looked strange. She sat upright. She took the child in her arms, she kissed it, and she offered it the breast. Then the horrible suspicion flashed across her mind that something had happened to the child. She tried to open its eyes with her fingers. She shook it violently, and she uttered that scream which Mrs. Dry says she shall never forget if she lives to the age of Methuselah.

Mrs. Dry sent for the doctor. He looked at the child, and as gently as he could, he told Mimmie it was dead. In his opinion it had been smothered whilst sleeping.

Another fortnight passes away. Mimmie has been delirious for nearly the whole of that period, but is now nearly well. Mr. Simpkin says she only requires a few days to recover her strength. While still excessively weak, Mimmie went out, and continued to do so daily. Mrs Dry, remarked that it was quite miraculous how Mimmie walked about after all she had gone through. She received another letter from William, asking her to meet him in the evening in the City. This was the occasion referred to in the evidence. They met, as we have intimated, and entered a cab. After driving out of the City, they left the cab, and began to walk. Hitherto not one word had Mimmie spoken. At last she found utterance, and told William all that had happened. For a moment even he felt remorse.

"William," she said, "I murdered the child."

He started from her, and exclaimed, "Murdered it, Mimmie!" She told him again the story of that night, and it was in vain that he tried to persuade her she was not guilty of the death of the child. The idea was fixed in her mind that she had murdered it in the hour of her madness. William told her it was no use indulging in foolish fancies, and that, perhaps, after all it was better the child was dead.

"Better it is dead!" said Mimmie, and she let go his arm, and stood looking at him as if she doubted whether she heard him aright.

"Don't look like that," said William, "I hate it."

"Better it is dead!" she exclaimed again.

"Yes," said William passionately; "and better if you were dead too, if you are going on like this."

"I shall trouble you no more," said Mimmie.

"As you like about that," rejoined William; "I told you we must part. The fact is I have been forced to marry!"

"So you are married!" said Mimmie, in a calm tone that jarred on the listener. "So you are married! that is well. I will trouble you no more. Good-bye, William, may you be happy!"

"Come" said William, "give me a kiss before we part;" but she heeded him not, and turned away.

She walked to the New Cut, and stood some time before Mrs. Dry's house, but would not enter it. She began walking quickly, not thinking where she was going. The words "Better it is dead" were still ringing in her ears as though William was by her side repeating them. She paused for awhile on Westminster-bridge, leant over the parapet, and looked on the darkly-flowing river. A policeman told her to move on, and she did so at once. She glided through the streets till she came to Hyde Park, which she entered. She felt very weary, and longed for rest. For the first time she noticed the coldness of the night, and perceived that snow was falling. Still she walked on, and leaving the main path lay down under a leafless tree, and she slept. She slept as she had not done for weeks past. She slept as if she was in the old home from which William had taken her. She slept as if she had not loved and been forsaken.

Next morning the park-keeper having breakfasted took a stroll by Rotten Row. He was attracted by a heap of snow gathered under one of the trees. He went up to it and kicked it, and found it was a woman lying there. He went to the hospital for assistance, telling them that one of the tramps, he thought, was "froze to death." A stretcher was brought, and all that remained on earth of Mimmie was carried to the hospital.

The coroner was notified of the event, and a jury was summoned to meet at the Red Lion public-house. Thirteen unfortunate men, including Mr. Trimmer, the greengrocer, assembled at the appointed time and rather irritated the beadle by insisting on partaking of some slight refreshment at the bar before entering the august presence of the coroner, who is popularly supposed to conduct the inquiry, but the *de facto* official is the beadle. The beadle summonses the jury, he gets up the evidence, and he tells witnesses what they are to say. The jury being sworn proceeded to view the body, which was a formal proceeding, inasmuch as the jurors took particular care to keep their eyes shut, and not to look at the corpse. The evidence that we have already mentioned was given, and the coroner charged the jury. Whilst he was doing so, Mr. Trimmer whispered to the foreman of the jury that if the cold wind continued he should be obliged to oil his hands, which were very much chapped and remarkably dirty.

The jury returned an open verdict of "Found dead," and the Coroner issued a certificate for Christian burial. The workhouse undertaker supplied a shell, and Mimmie was buried at the expense of the parish.

Found dead! How often these open verdicts are returned! How many people from year to year die in the streets of London, unfriended and uncared for! What tales of utter woe and wretchedness are summed up in those two words FOUND DEAD!

CONSTABLE'S HOTEL.

———o———

A DIRTY-LOOKING LETTER and twopence to pay. Give it back to the postman. We are not to be done by the begging-letter imposters, who, as a proof of their utter destitution, omit to frank their appeals to the benevolent. If a friend has forgotten to affix the countenance of the Queen, it will serve him right to get his letter returned for his carelessness. Still, never mind, we will pay the twopence this time, for it would be rather vexatious to send back a pleasant invitation. This is what we had for our two-pence :—

Constable's Hotel, Tuesday Night.

My dear Friend,—You will be surprised to hear that I am somewhat in debt, and that a creditor has been heartless enough to arrest me. I am not sorry for it, for now I will take the bull by the horns and go through the Court. I will now get rid of that burden which for years past has been a drag upon my career, and a spell upon my intellect. Hereafter, of course, I mean to pay all my creditors, but the brute who has put me in prison shall be the last I will settle with. Give me a call at once, as I have something in hand more important than a hundred bankruptcies.

Ever yours,
In sunshine and shade,
DAN. BRADY.

P.S.—Bring some tobacco and pipes. The brutes do not allow spirits. I presume that you know that Constable's Hotel is the polite name for Whitecross-street Prison.

We were not surprised to hear of Brady being in debt, as he had always been in that condition from his youth upwards We were, indeed, a little surprised that a creditor should think it worth while to sue a gentleman of such notorious impecuniosity. However, we were determined to lose no time in visiting our friend, who was, from the tone of his letter, evidently down upon his luck. No wonder, poor fellow! Cut off from his beloved whiskey, what could be expected but gloominess?

We hail a cab, and request to be driven to Cripplegate. The cabman said "All right," in a patronizing tone which was slightly irritating. It indicated that he knew that we were going to the prison, confound the fellow! We pulled the check string rather sharply, and told him to stop at a tobacconist's. Whilst we were investing in bird's-eye and half-a-dozen short pipes, Cabby walked in to light up. "They likes the weed," he remarked, "it's meat, drink and family to 'em." We asked how he knew. "Bless my eyes and yourn," he replied, "I've served my time in that shop, like other gents. I was one too many for the Governor, though, I was; and I can just put you up to a move, sir. Spirits is against the rules, but I had 'em all the same. My old woman comes in twice a week with a big pie. In course they let that pass; and in course, under the crust were a bottle of the real stuff. Best of the fun was this 'ere. I gets rayther tight, and in the morning was like a 'oss off his legs. Round comes the doctor, and 'as a squint at me. 'What have you been eating?' says he. I told him the old woman brought me in pies which were uncommon fat, and I missed the qualifier. Blest if the doctor wornt a good sort of chap, for he orders me a leetle brandy."

The tobacconist having enjoyed the joke, and offered Cabby a cheroot, the price of which he deducted out of our change, the journey was resumed. We pass down Jewin-street, which is singularly suggestive of genteel penury; we pass by Cripplegate Church, which is the most nondescript and unsightly edifice ever dedicated to Divine worship, and, turning sharp round to the left, we pull up at the prison door. Cabby tips us another patronizing wink as he drives off. What does he mean by that sort of thing? Has he got some cloudy notion about surrendering to one's bankruptcy, and does he think that we have been so obliging as to arrest ourselves?

Did you ever go to prison? There is a nasty creeping sort of feeling comes over us even when entering one as a visitor. We look through the wicket. A tall warder opens the door with a jangle of the keys, and as soon as we are on the wrong side, closes it with a bang that seems to say, "Caged my boy, during Her Majesty's pleasure." We told the warder we wanted to see Mr. Daniel Brady.

"Have you got anything for him?"

We muttered something about tobacco and pipes.

"Have you got any spirits?" asked the warder, eyeing us suspiciously.

Our "No" did not satisfy him, for he passed his heavy hand over our coat, and then told us to go on. We passed through a passage, barred up on either side, and came to another gate. Another jangling of keys and another discordant bang. We enter the main building, and at the end of a short dark passage we come upon the reception-room. Some more jangling of keys, and we are locked in the said reception room while the warder calls for our friend.

Reception room! Dreary, dirty, and dilapidated. A double row of narrow wooden tables, flanked by narrow wooden benches. No ventilation. On one side of the room a stove, but no fire in it. The room is demi-semi lighted by demi-semi-translucent windows, looking into the prisoners' court-yard, where some of the prisoners were playing at ball. What practical advantage the community derives, and especially creditors, from debtors having to play ball, and being kept in a state of enforced idleness, we could not discover. Imprisonment for debt is clearly not intended as a punishment, and therefore is, we suppose, preserved as a curious relic of ancestral folly.

Enter Brady, rather grimy, but otherwise none the worse for incarceration.

"By Gad, my dear friend, this affects me. I knew you would come. I was just telling my solicitor you would be here."

After the usual "how-do-you-do" and "weather" dialogue, Brady told us that he hoped to be out in a few days, and that in an hour he was going to Basinghall-street to file his papers.

"You see, my dear boy, I am going to do the business *in forma pauperis*, which costs next to nothing. A fellow can only do that when he has no assets. Therefore if a chap wants to be let through easily he should not have a stick to call his own. Plenty of debts and no assets is the correct thing."

Rather a sharp-looking man whose dress was showy and sloppy, and whose jewellery was conspicuous if not valuable, called Brady inside. After a minute's chat this person was introduced to us as " Mr. Recker, my solicitor."

"My dear friend," said Brady "my solicitor wants some money before he can proceed."

"Indeed!"

"I am in no hurry," said Mr. Recker "but as I told you yesterday we cannot file to-day unless I get two guineas on account."

"My dear friend," said Brady "could you oblige with the amount? I will repay you next Monday." Ever since we have known Brady his pay-day has been " next Monday." We handed over the money to Mr. Recker, who dropped it gracefully into his waistcoat pocket, and told Brady to be ready for a start in half an hour.

We inquired of Brady how he got on in prison.

"Oh, jolly enough. I have pleasant chums and the sleeping is pretty good. The miseries are having to go to bed early, to get up ditto, to go to chapel, and no spirits allowed."

"Spirits again! Brady wrote to us about spirits. Our one-time insolvent Cabby talked to us about spirits. The warder searched us for spirits, and Brady at once reverts to spirits. It seems to be the bone of contention, and the sole object at Whitecross street, for the officials to try to keep the prisoners from drinking ardent spirits and for the prisoners to try to get spirits to drink. The prisoners appear to succeed, thanks to the thirsty weakness of the warders.

"But," said Brady "we manage to get a pretty fair supply of the creature comfort."

"How?"

"Oh, many ways. Milk, for example."

"Milk?"

"Well, we are allowed milk. Milk has to be brought in cans. It is easy enough to drown a bottle of the needful in a milk can."

Brady told us that there were some noble fellows in the prison—men of the right sort, and well off, too. " Yes, my dear friend, there is an officer to whom I shall introduce you. He has plenty of money, but somehow or other he gets in here to settle. Well, it is with him I have met with surprising luck. I tell you, my friend, what I would not mention to another living soul. The captain is going to start a newspaper for the purpose of upsetting the Horse Guards, and I am to be the editor. If you like to write for it, do so. Money is no object, and you shall have your four guineas an article, and write as many articles as you like. Is not Providence good to me?"

Brady was not jesting. No matter how visionary a scheme, he would believe it. He was a victim of that most fatal of all social diseases—unlimited sanguineness. A word was enough to persuade him that he was on the eve of obtaining a splendid fortune, and he would not have been surprised to receive at any moment an autograph letter from the Queen, asking him to form a Cabinet, or to become Commander-in-Chief. Brady was perpetually answering advertisements, and, after a thousand disappointments, he was quite confident that he should get the appointment for which he applied. Another peculiarity of Brady's was his idea of Providence. If he was depressed—he was so now and then for a few hours—he said Providence was against him. If he was cheerful, that is, if he was indulging in castle-building—which he did night and day—he said Providence was doing wonders for him. He had a half-defined impression that Providence would suspend any laws, and work any number of miracles, for the sake of Daniel Brady. We are not finding any fault with our friend. He was benevolent, without the slightest discrimination or judgment. All his male acquaintances, no matter what their shortcomings, were—particularly if they were penniless—godlike souls, and all his female acquaintances were noble and divine women. He lives in a delusive dream from which no experience ever awakens him.

Whilst Brady went to prepare for the walk to Basinghall-street we had time to look round the room, which was tolerably full of visitors. Some were laughing, and others were sad. Here was a wife talking about the affairs of home, and there was a daughter trying to look calm, but who would have a cry when she reached home. Will some one be good enough to tell us what is the good of this imprisonment for debt? It is true, it is not for long—for not more than a few days or at most a few weeks. It is true if a man is vigilant, he can file his own petition, get protection from arrest, and so avoid Constable's Hotel. It is true that a short imprisonment is the precursor of freedom from debt. But why this short imprisonment? Does it benefit the creditors? We grant that it hurts the debtors. The few days or few weeks of imprisonment, unfit a man for work, and produce a feeling of recklessness. What saith Brady? "My dear friend, if fellows knew how easy it is, they would not mind debt, and, instead of working hard to pay their creditors, would snap their fingers at them." Suppose, instead of imprisonment, a bankrupt, after seven years was compelled to give an account of his then property, and that, say, one-third of it had to be divided amongst his creditors. We take it that such an arrangement would be of advantage to the creditors, it would not discourage the exertions of the honest debtor, and, as for the dishonest debtor, it signifies not whether he is or is not discouraged.

We went with Brady, escorted by a warder, to Basinghall-street, making a call, *en route*, at a public-house, for a drink — spirits, of course. At Basinghall-street we met

Mr. Recker. We went into a room in which were seated two gentlemen—registrars. One was reading a newspaper, and the other was doing business. Brady, without reading, signed several papers put before him by Mr. Recker, and then swore to the truth of their contents. Next he went up-stairs into an office nominally to surrender his property, but as he had no property to surrender, we presume he swore that he had none. On our way back to Whitecross-street there was another call at the public-house, where the warder and Brady liquored up, and the latter procured a dram bottle of spirits, which he concealed in his trousers. As we passed through the railed passage above referred to we asked the warder who were the prisoners confined in the large iron cage on our left. We were told that they were County Court prisoners. The majority of them were working men, and were in their working dress. Where were their families?

This is the County Court system in practice:—A debtor is ordered to pay so much a week or a month, at the discretion of the judge. If he neglects to do so he is again summoned, and the judge may at his discretion commit him for a period of not more than forty days, for what is facetiously called contempt of court. But the imprisonment does not pay the debt. Let us take the case of a labourer who has a hard time of it. He gets into debt with his baker for, say, eighteen shillings. He is summoned to the County Court. He is ordered to pay, and does not. He is sent to prison, and in the meantime his family are deprived of all honest means of support. At the end of the ten, or twenty, or thirty, or forty days he comes out of prison. After a little while he is summoned for the same debt, and may go to prison for the same debt again and again. Is this just? Is this not a gross and glaring iniquity? Why should a man, because he owes less than twenty pounds, be imprisoned for any period not exceeding forty days, and yet this imprisonment not release him from his debt, whilst the man who owes large debts may avoid imprisonment altogether, or, if he is arrested, will get out in less than forty days and all his debts be cancelled?

We shall be told, forsooth, about the contempt of court. We shall be told that the judge only commits when the debtor can and yet will not pay. How can and will not pay? Has he property? Then seize it for his debt. Oh no he may not have property, but he has wages and he ought to pay out of his earnings. Are the working classes the only earners of money? Why not apply the same rule to the large debtors? Why not compel them under penalty of repeated imprisonments to set apart some of their earnings for their creditors? That would not do. The object of insolvent legislation is to relieve the debtor of the burden that presses upon him and keeps him down. An admirable principle. It is politic if a man gives up all he has to allow him to start again free from debt. But why not apply the admirable principle to the poor debtor? Why, when a working man has given up all he has, are his future earnings to be taxed for the payment of his debts under the penalty of constantly recurring imprisonment if he does not or cannot pay the sum ordered by the County Court judge? No legal sophistry can get over the fact of that iron cage at Constable's Hotel, filled with working men who have given up all their property, who are imprisoned from time to time at the discretion of a judge, but whose imprisonment does not relieve them from their debts. A gentleman owes his tradesmen—tailors, bootmakers, and it may be jewellers—£500. He goes to Constable's Hotel for a week or two, and in less than two months he is free from debt. Next year he may come into a large property, or he may be earning £500 a year, but there is no legal obligation on him to pay his old creditors. A bricklayer owes one pound for meat or bread. He goes to prison for a fortnight, but he does not wipe off his debt. Next month he gets work. He begins to recover a little from the difficulties incident to his enforced idleness. Again there is a little fire in the grate, his children are beginning to be clothed, and they are no longer tormented with the pangs of hunger. Down comes his old creditor on him, and the judge issues an order for two shillings a week. What wonder that the man becomes indifferent and gives up the struggle in despair? This is not a fancy picture. Go to Whitecross-street prison, genteelly called Constable's Hotel. Look at the working men in the iron cage on the left. The big debtor who gets into prison is ever after free from his creditors, for the law will not permit the creditor to touch his future earnings or even his future property. For the poor debtor there is no such mercy. He must give up all he has, and yet his future earnings are mortgaged to his creditors. If a gentleman owes £500, his debts are forgiven him. If a working man owes one pound for bread or meat, there is no forgiveness. Verily, in this instance, there is one law for the rich debtor and quite another law for the poor debtor, and the sooner there is an end to the distinction the better. We cannot forget those working men in working dress in the iron-cage at Whitecross-street prison.

"MARY ANNE," A1 FOR EVER.

THE most commonplace ruins in the world are the ruins of Rochester Castle. There is not a vestige of romance about them. There is no appearance of antiquity or evidence of decay. One would suppose that the Castle had been gutted by a fire which had consumed everything but the bare walls, or that it had always been an unfinished building. Yet from frequent visits to the place we began to like it, and now that the solitude is peopled with past personal recollections, there is some question in our mind whether the grim remains of Rochester Castle are not preferable to Tintern Abbey. It was in Rochester Castle we first met our dear and valued friend, Captain Roberts, of the *Mary Anne*. The gallant Captain, who appeared remarkably like a fish out of water, was lolling in the courtyard cracking nuts, and throwing the shells at the walls, perhaps to test their strength. Very fortunately Captain Roberts missed his aim with one shell, which, instead of striking the wall, struck our cheek, and the incident led to an acquaintance, which fast ripened into friendship.

Captain Roberts was about as an unnautical a looking man as can well be conceived. He was tall, thin, and walked without the slightest rolling. His conversation was as free from sea phrases as though he had been a landlubber from youth upwards. Captain Roberts was not in her Majesty's service, nor was he exactly in the merchant service. He was the owner and commander of the *Mary Anne*, a decked fishing-boat, of something less than twenty tons register. A daintier little craft than the *Mary Anne* never sailed out of Rochester. Her lines were not particularly striking; but her speed was the wonder and envy of rival fishermen. Many a time has the *Mary Anne* put to shame some of the yachts belonging to the crack clubs. Moreover the *Mary Anne* was an eminently neat and spruce craft. No Dutch vessel that ever sailed was freer from untidiness and uncleanliness. Her crew consisted of Captain Roberts and a boy. At least, we suppose the crew was a boy—a regular young giant, with the sturdiest of limbs, and a complexion of the hue of the setting sun.

Our friendship with Captain Roberts resulted in the *Mary Anne* becoming for all practical purposes our yacht. During the season, as often as we could, we used to go out in her, generally hugging the coast, but not unfrequently paying a visit to the opposite shore. It was a jolly though not an eventful life on board the *Mary Anne*. Here is the log for a day: About five in the morning the captain gives a cheerful "Ay, ay, sir!" and we get up, and go on deck, and the boy—he had no other name than the boy—threw out a sail under the direction of the captain, and we plunged into "the briny," and had a glorious bath. Our ablutions over, the next business was breakfast, which consisted of coffee without milk, cold fried fish and the inevitable pipe. The morning was devoted to cruising about lazily, comfortably, and with an inexpressible kind of pleasure. There is a joy in being on the big sea in a little craft, which must be felt, but cannot be described. Every vessel that we met was duly examined by the aid of the glass, and her build criticised. Sometimes we essayed to learn the art of practical navigation, but we signally failed. Captain Roberts was too discreet a mariner ever to trust his vessel to our charge. About eleven o'clock our labours commenced. We were the cook of the vessel. The fact is Captain Roberts was profoundly ignorant of the culinary art. The boy was pretty well up in plain cooking, but his hands were objectionable. We are by no means dainty; yet we disliked our food being pulled about by hands that were of the colour of red ochre very much soiled indeed.

Whether the boy ever washed his hands we know not; but we do know that whenever we saw them they were grimy, and that under the nails there was a landed estate of no inconsiderable dimensions. So we became cook, with the approbation of Captain Roberts and to the amusement of the boy. Without any desire to blow our own trumpet, we conscientiously aver that we do not think that even Soyer could have done better than we did with the materials at our command. Our fried fish rivalled the fried fish one meets with in Houndsditch, and our puddings were inimitable. Rather heavy, perhaps, and slightly doughy, but we never spared the plums. At all events, if the proof of the pudding is in the quantity eaten, our puddings were superlatively good. The boy devoured them by the pound at the time, and his ostrich-like digestion was by no means impared. After dinner the Captain and we did the sociable. We smoked, and Roberts cracked nuts. We believe Roberts ate more nuts than any other person in the world. He ate them, too, in a deliberate sailor-like manner. The walnut was slowly drawn from his pocket. Then it was examined and rubbed on the knee. Next it was crushed between the captain's fingers, the shells were gently tossed into the sea, every particle of skin was removed, the nut was slipped into the left-hand waistcoat pocket, in which Roberts always carried salt, and then, being fully prepared, it was jerked into the mouth and masticated with the utmost deliberation and with manifest enjoyment. There was not much conversation. Roberts was rather taciturn, and his stories, few in number, were not particularly lively. But though we did not talk much, the afternoons were sociable. The boy was also silent, except when he saw, or fancied he saw, something extraordinary in the way of fish. As no one paid the slightest regard to his remarks, they did not interrupt the dumb harmony of the meeting. Towards evening there was another meal of fish and coffee, followed by a glass of grog. When darkness covered the face of the deep we came to anchor. Our flag was lowered, and we were gently rocked to sleep by the motion of the waves. The cabin was very small, so that in lying down we were obliged to bring knees and chin into unnaturally close quarters. But at eighteen one cares not for such trifling inconveniences. At that age the body is as supple as the heart is light.

We had our gala days. Sometimes we shipped a landsman and enjoyed his misery. A Cockney at sea is about the most wretched animal on the face of the earth, and is fair sport for the sea dogs. Occasionally we did a little— a very little—smuggling for brandy and tobacco. In the season the *Mary Anne* was in a sailing match, and more than once carried off the prize. Roberts was very proud of his trophies, but not more so than was his wife.

A kinder soul than Mrs. Roberts never lived. A buxom, winsome, and motherly wife, that it does one good to know and to remember. Such a clever woman, too! How beautifully she managed Roberts! He reigned—she ruled; and he, innocent man, thought he both ruled and reigned. A neater cottage than the "Laurels" was not to be found in the three kingdoms. It was situated at Erith, in Kent, at which place Roberts lived, because his fathers had done so before him. Erith in those days was a pleasant country village. Now it is covered with villas. Then everybody knew everybody else. Now everybody is too proper to know anybody else. "Love your neighbour as yourself," enjoins the Bible. "Let your neighbours be as strangers unto you," is the edict of modern gentility. On Saturdays Roberts always went home, and remained at home until the Monday, and we were delighted to accompany him. The captain, after tea and gossip, made boats for the youngsters, and Mrs. Roberts did the washing and the mending. A handy woman with her needle was Mrs. Roberts. She made most of her husband's clothes and all her children's clothes. She rather disgusted the son and heir—a sturdy boy, seven years' old —by running tucks in his corduroys; but, as she remarked, it was necessary to allow for growing. She made one pair of trousers the same before as behind, so that when the knees became shabby they could be turned about. We gave the *coup de grace* to this ingenious device by an Hibernian, telling her the lad would not know whether he was going forwards or backwards, and would be innocently playing the truant by walking home instead of to school. After the children had been put to bed, came the supper—a hot, substantial supper—and this was followed by pipes and grog. The captain and ourselves took whisky, whilst Mrs. Roberts took gin, the stimulant that most ladies like best, though they are not all candid enough to admit the preference. We usually drank to "sweethearts and wives," and indulged in some banter, of which the captain was the willing subject and butt. Before retiring for the night we were assured—a needless assurance—that the sheets were well aired, and that our bed was ditto, because two of the children had been sleeping in it all the week.

The Sunday was a quiet, happy day. In the morning Mrs. Roberts insisted upon all going to church except herself and the youngest children. The exigencies of the dinner and the baby kept her at home. It was an old church and an old-fashioned service. The vicar was an aged man and not remarkable for attention to his parish, but rather notorious for his negligence. He was on intimate terms with the jolly old lord who lived on the top of a hill close by—and both the lord and the parson were two bottle men. Often, and often, has the service been delayed until the said lord had entered the church. The sermons were peculiarly sleepy, but happily short. They had been preached over and over again for forty years. The captain was attentive enough during the prayers, but the sermon was an awful trial of patience. He kept himself awake by tying hard knots in his handkerchief and untying them with his teeth. In the afternoon the family went out for a walk unless the *Mary Anne* happened to be in the Reach, and then there was a sail. This did not please the boy who was always rated by Mrs. Roberts for not being clean.

The captain was wont to tell her that the boy was the right sort, and the invariable reply was "I dare say he is, but I tell you he is a regular heathen."

After a few, a very few years, to our lasting regret, we lost our friends. And this is how it happened. Whenever the boating season came round we found that Mrs. Roberts was in an interesting condition, or that she had lately been in an interesting condition. There was always a new baby or a new baby shortly expected. Now those events, which in palaces tend to strengthen the attachment to the throne, are rather serious when they occur frequently in cottages. They are blessings no doubt, but they are expensive blessings. Mrs. Roberts with the eighth pledge of affection lying in her lap, told us that the family was so large that something must be done. She could no longer save a penny; and, indeed, had been compelled to draw upon the savings to meet the expenditure incidental to the last event. What was to become of the children, as they grew up? How were they to be put out in the world? Father would not always be young, and able to work as he now worked. So Mrs. Roberts thought of going to Australia, where, with what they had saved, they could get a farm, and might be able to do in the world. What did we think of the plan.

We did not like it, and the bare thought of losing our friends, made us feel discontented and savage. But what could be said against it? Most ungraciously we confessed that the plan was good, and forthwith Mrs. Roberts set about putting it into execution. Before the summer was over—it was a dull summer—the happy home was sold, the *Mary Anne* was sold, the money was drawn from the savings' bank, places were engaged in an emigrant ship, and with enough to start them fairly, the Robertses went to Australia.

The parting day is not to be forgotten. There is not, to our thinking, any sadder sight than an emigrant ship. The vessel was moored off Gravesend. The Robertses had gone on board the night before the day of sailing, and in the morning we went on board to say farewell. It was a scene of confusion that baffles description. The deck was littered with packages and ropes. The passengers were in the way of the sailors, and the sailors were in the way of the passengers. There were parents saying good-bye to their children, and friends parting with friends, perhaps for years—most likely for ever. Wherever we looked there were sorrowing faces, and above the din of preparation were heard the sounds of lamentation. Those who had no friends present—they were best off—were listlessly watching the sailors at work, or staring at the shore. The Robertses were as much cast down as people can be who are doing that which is right. Oh, it is a bitter trial to go away for ever and for ever from the land of one's birth. We had thought over some words of consolation and kindly farewell, but we forgot them, or they stuck in our throat. We looked at the cabin, we talked a little about the weather, and we promised to write frequently. " If I does well I will come back to the old country, and see you before I go on the long, long voyage," said Roberts. " We shall never do that," sobbed Mrs. Roberts, " we shall never do that. I wish I had never done this thing." Roberts looked wistfully towards the shore. " It ain't too late now," he muttered. The children came about him, and the momentary feeling of despair passed away. Then we sat down in a group, and we counted the leaden minutes. We had no wish to part, yet we all wished the parting scene over. It was a relief to hear that the pilot was on board. It was a relief to hear the order for all strangers to go on shore.

We heard that order and obeyed it promptly. " I wish you had not come to-day," cried Mrs. Roberts, " and oh, I wish I had not done this thing." We kissed the children, who wondered what father and mother and " nunky"—that was the name they called us—were so grieved about. We embraced Mrs. Roberts, not attempting to utter a word of farewell. Grasping Roberts's honest hand, and with a God bless you, we parted. As the boat by which we left the ship neared the shore, we ventured to look up. There were the Robertses, signalling farewell; and we waved our handkerchief in return. And so we parted, never to meet again on this earth, with the captain of the *Mary Anne*, and with his good and noble wife. Perhaps we may be laughed at for loving so well a fisherman and his wife. Perhaps we may be sneered at for yachting in a fishing-smack. We are proud to own our respect and affection for an honest man and a true womanly woman; and the *Mary Anne*—dear old craft!—will, in our memory, be rated A 1 for ever.

EASTER MONDAY.

———o———

In London the gentility stops at home on Easter Monday. It is the holiday of the toiling millions, and they make the most of it. Early in the morning the railway stations are thronged with excursionists. Some are going to favourite retreats in the neighbourhood of the metropolis. Others are going to do Brighton and back, with eight hours at the sea-side, for three shillings. Richmond, Kew, and Hampton Court are extensively patronised. Gravesend will do a considerable trade in shrimps. And when all the world has gone out of town what a great world remains in town! The streets are thronged with men, women and children seeking pleasure. They saunter about staring at the shops, staring at the lamp-posts, and staring at vacancy. Every one to his taste. The streets of London are, perhaps, agreeable to holiday folk, and moreover even a cheap excursion costs money. Well, then, is it not prudent for those who are poor and frugal-minded to give up the idea of an excursion and so better afford a visit to the theatre in the evening? There is another reason why so many remain in town. We often read advertisements for a married couple without " incumbrances"—yes, that is the word. What a satire on our civilization! What a satire, and what a coarse, bitter, ugly fact! Amend the dictionary as follows:—

" Children.—The young offspring of rich people."

" Incumbrances.—The young offspring of poor people."

But in one sense they are incumbrances on Easter Monday. Supposing there is not a young baby and a little toddler, and suppose the incumbrances are old enough to go out, an excursion is still impossible. When you come to multiply three shillings by six and add to it the extras, also multiplied by six, you have a sum total that represents more than a week's earnings in the best season. Therefore on Easter Monday the streets of London are crowded with families. Father and mother, and the little ones, clinging to each other as if they were somebodies, and not mere machines and incumbrances. Look at that stalwart mechanic—the model and perfection of a working man. There is a slight stoop about the shoulders, and he saunters along with a sort of indolent, heavy languor. But look at him closely. What a giant he will be to-morrow when he wields the hammer or stands at the vice! Shrewd, clever men are the mechanics of England. They manage their class affairs with consummate tact, and in the contest with capital come off victorious. But they have not read, or do not believe in the Malthusian philosophy. They marry early, and get children as fast as they can. Nor are they ashamed of their incumbrances. Glance again at our sauntering Vulcan. He is carrying the baby! " Very unmanly," says the exquisite. Poor Fitz-Noodle! If you could look a little below the surface you would be induced to envy rather than despise that mechanic. Is it not something—a pretty big something—to have a wife who loves you, and children who think of you as a father, and not merely as a governor to be bled pecuniarily? Incredible as it may seem to you, Fitz-Noodle, the mechanic is so blessed, and you—well, you are only a chattel or part, and not the most important part, of a marriage settlement. There, Fitz-Noodle, go home. What do you out on Easter Monday? Have you forgotten " The Genteel Catechism?" Use the working classes for your profit by all means. Write books about them, if you are minded to bring down the price of waste paper. Send missionaries to the labouring classes to preach to them and to teach them. But you must not mix with them, neither in the park, nor in the street; not in the theatre, nor in the church. Note how careful the Church is to practically inculcate " the Genteel Catechism." Genteel sinners sit in comfortable pews, whilst vulgar sinners are huddled together in free seats. And now, Fitz-Noodle, is the great festival of Christianity. The Church celebrates the crowning work of Redemption. Is it right at such a time to forget the Genteel Catechism? You will be startled to hear, Fitz-Noodle, that on the Continent, at such seasons, high and low, rich and poor, meet together. Ah, happy and proper London! Gentility stops at home when the toiling millions make holiday.

We—forgive the delinquency, oh! genteel friends—will take a trip down the river as far as Greenwich. How many passengers the steamers are licensed to carry we know not, but they carry enough to add a spice of danger to the other excitements of the voyage. Here we are on board, the rope is let go, and we are off. We shoot through the arches of London-bridge, and enter the Pool. Delightful! Talk about the Rhine, or for the matter of that, the Mississippi! We grant the Mississippi is bigger, but it was not dug out, so do not, dear American cousins, bawl too loudly of its bigness. What port can vie with the port of London in its show of shipping? The band—a fiddle and a harp—strikes up "Rule Britannia," and our patriotism is so stirred within us that we bestow upon the said band a liberal donation of copper coins.

The passengers are jolly. The lasses are dressed in their best, and it is amusing to observe how nearly they copy the toilets of Belgravia—in style we mean, not in quality. We have no wish to be hypercritical, but it seems to us that some of the damsels have made too free use of their mistress's pearl powder and rouge, that their hair is too much bandolined, and that their gloves are about three sizes too small. It is rather painful to see reeves of red flesh overlapping the tops of the gloves. The fair ones are for the most part accompanied by the young men with whom they are keeping company. The cavaliers are also fashionably attired. Patent leather boots, at seven and sixpence, warranted not to come to pieces the first time of wearing them, light trousers, of last season's cut, waistcoats of conspicuous patterns, coats of cloth that in a photograph looks as good as the best West of England, and shiny hats. The gentlemen for the most part carry their gloves in their pockets, so that their resplendent rings are not hidden by thread or kid. Ah, but we have omitted an all-important item. The gentlemen are smoking cigars or cheroots. No girl who has a notion of what things ought to be would keep company with a young man who did not smoke on Sundays and holidays. What the cigars and cheroots are made of we know not, but we opine that they are a mixture of English cabbage and of German tobacco, which tobacco is vastly inferior to English cabbage. Happily for our olfactory nerves, the men who are not keeping company smoke American tobacco in pipes.

Before we get out of the Pool baskets are opened, and there is a general consumption of food, principally sandwiches—substantial sandwiches, at least an inch and a half in thickness. Those who are not provided with home liquors drink stout, which is frothy and of excellent quality on the Thames steamers. The favourite beverage, however, is gin and water hot, with plenty of lemon. "Oh," said a lady who was eating voraciously, "'aint it plummy? I'se so enjoying myself!" We beg to explain that the lady was not guilty of self-cannibalism. She was not eating her own flesh, but eel-pies, and she was carefully spitting away the bones.

Greenwich! Such a pushing to get out of the boat, as if life and happiness depended upon being the first to land. The eel-pie lady was squeamish, and required a little guiding along the landing-stage. The river was not rough, but eel-pies and hot gin and water sweet are of a somewhat bilious tendency.

Greenwich Fair is a thing of the past. Some one found out that fairs were immoral, and so they have been put down. But the park has not yet been abolished by the reformers, and to that we proceed. Here are all sorts of games, to suit all tastes. Running, jumping, Aunt Sally, kiss-in-the-ring, dancing to accordions and fiddles, eating and

I

drinking on the grass, and running down the famous Greenwich hill. The said hill is not large, but it is steepish, and the sport consists in having a tumble every third or fourth run. Such tumbling would break the limbs and concuss the brain of a genteel body, but is does not hurt the holiday folk. It is a merry scene. Shouting, screaming, talking, and boisterous laughter. Fitz-Noodle, if it were lawful, it would do you good to witness it.

Leaving the park, we proceed through the streets of Greenwich. At every house is a woman touting for customers. Tea, with shrimps, for ninepence a-head. Tea, with shrimps, and private rooms for parties, at a shilling a-head. That sounds cheap, and it is cheap. Those who avail themselves of the bargain do not fail to clear up the bread and butter, and shrimps, and to empty the sugar basin. Running in the park, singing choruses, and boisterous laughing, are exceedingly provocative of appetite. If you will eschew eel-pies and hot gin-and-water, you will find, my afflicted friend, that an Easter Monday excursion to Greenwich is a more effectual cure for dyspepsia than blue pill.

We return to town by railway, and have a hard battle to get a seat in a carriage. All distinctions of class are, for the nonce, forgotten. No matter what your class, get in where you can, and as a rule, the third-class passengers get into first-class carriages, and the first-class passengers get into third-class carriages.

So far, the Easter Monday picture is pleasant enough. Is there not a dark side?

We will not finish by going to the theatre. We decline to visit the music-halls. We will, on the suggestion of a friend, enter a casino, and tell as much about it as may be told without offence.

A large hall with galleries running round it, handsomely decorated and gaily lighted. A band that plays dance music well. Nearly all the women are of the *demi-monde*. The men are of several classes. There is the genteel *roue* who sits in the gallery and smokes, and would not dance for any amount of money. There is the old *roue*, whose evil passions have outlived his prime of years. There is the young man who dances. He is either a hundred-and-fifty-pound-a-year clerk, or a shopman. His dress is fast, and his face dissipated and unwholesome. Examine these dancing men, and you will see at once that they are not an intellectual class. If they have any brains at all they are in their legs. No man with a fair intellect is a great dancer. Besides the classes here referred to, there are a sprinkling of decent men and women, who go to the casino out of curiosity, and we are told that on Easter Monday the number of decent visitors is larger than usual.

The dancing is orderly, thanks to the exertions of the persons who act as masters of the ceremonies. Orderly, but not refined. To write plainly, the dancing is grossly immodest; and it is the immodesty that attracts the audience in the galleries. Quadrilles do not seem to be much in vogue, but polkas and waltzes are in constant demand.

It was pitiable to see the decent girls joining in these performances. You could distinguish them at a glance from the *demi-monde*. The friend who took us into the place assured us that the London casinos do more to promote London prostitution than any other institution. We can readily believe him. No man who has a vestige of manly love or respect for a girl would take her to such a place, and no girl can visit such a place even once without weakening that self-respect which is one of virtue's strongest bulwarks.

Look at that girl who is taking some refreshment after a dance. Pretty, is she not? The face is painted, but even through the paint we can trace a kind countenance. What she is in moral character is too perceptible; and we learn from our friend what she was but a few, a very few, years ago. She was a pretty and virtuous girl. Not virtuous only in the sense that she had not fallen into sin, but virtuous in the highest sense—that is, that she was above the thought of vice. How did she fall? The story may be told in a few words, and it is so common a story that it is hardly worth the telling. She had to get her living. She went into a house of business. She was thrown into the society of men who looked upon her as their lawful prey. For a while she stood aloof, but by little and by little she relaxed in her demeanour. She became freer in her conversation. She permitted the son of her master to see her home. She went out with him. She, not knowing the customs of society, dreamt that the man would marry her. She knew not that genteel society will banish a gentleman who marries a girl who has to earn her daily bread by daily toil, but that genteel society does not think any the worse of a gentleman for seducing a girl who is so situated. So it came to pass that the girl fell, and there was one more added to the fifty or sixty thousand fallen women of London. That was all.

Let us away from this place. It has spoilt our Easter Monday excursion. Oh, this night-side of life! Oh, this too, too common story, that makes the whole heart sick! Sick for sheer pity's sake, and sick unto death when we think of sister or of daughter; and think, oh God, that but for an accidental superior social *status* they would be exposed to like temptation, and to a like fate. It is not good to dwell too much on the night-side of life. We get weary, and almost despair. We are almost overwhelmed with the falsity, the corruption, and misery that everywhere surrounds us. Better turn away from scenes of evil and of sadness. Better persuade the heart that affection is not a myth—that friendship is not a sham. You that have sisters or daughters, let your Easter Monday's excursion end with daylight; or, at least, do not look upon casino life. Do not so, unless your heart is seared and void of all compassion.

OUR DOMESTIC SERVANTS.

———o———

"WALK IN, LADIES! Walk in and select from the largest stock in the metropolis. We have always on hand an unfailing supply of the best and cheapest human flesh and blood."

Ah, do not be alarmed! I am not going to introduce you to a negro slave mart. Faugh! Negro flesh, forsooth! My dear lady, we are in London; and in London, you know, a slave block is not to be found. I refer to the sale not of negro, but to the hire of Caucasian, flesh and blood.

We enter a Servants' bazaar. We will accompany Mrs. Bashaw, who has come to do business. In a sort of wooden den or office is the man that takes the money. If you want a wet nurse the fee is five shillings; ditto for a cook; and for all other servants, including dry-nurses and housemaids, the fee is half-a-crown. Mrs. Bashaw wants a general servant, and therefore, for the privilege of selection, pays half-a-crown. The bazaar is divided into compartments. In one place the wet-nurses are railed off. In another the cooks are penned up. In another the housemaids, dry-nurses, and general servants are huddled together waiting to be hired.

Mrs. Bashaw being seated in a comfortably-furnished room, the female superintendent of the department waits upon her to ascertain her requirements. Mrs. Bashaw explains that she keeps a nurse, that she has a boy who cleans the knives and boots and assists in waiting, and that she wants a general servant who can cook. She must not be younger than twenty-one, or older than thirty. She must be tall and respectable-looking. She must have a long and unimpeachable character from her last place. She must be good-tempered, honest, sober, industrious, and obliging. Wages, eleven pounds a year, with a rise of a pound a year, if the girl does her duty. The female superintendent has no doubt that she will be able to suit her customer.

For a few minutes Mrs. Bashaw is left alone, and then enters a girl about four feet two. "Oh, you are too little," exclaims Mrs. Bashaw, and the girl retires. The next piece of goods is tall, but manifestly past forty. "It is no use asking you any questions," says Mrs. Bashaw, "you are too old." The next applicant is neither short nor old, but rather pale. "You are not healthy or strong enough for my place," says Mrs. Bashaw. The next comer is a likely-looking girl. Mrs. Bashaw asks her a few questions, and all is satisfactory until the question as to character is put. A good deal of blushing and a thickness of utterance, as if the girl had a bullet lodged in her throat. Her last mistress cannot deny that she was an honest and a good servant, but ——"Well, and why did you leave?" "Oh, ma'm," replied the girl sobbing, "I was so cruelly deceived, and oh, ma'm, I had a 'misfortune.'" Here, quick, bring in some disinfecting fluid. The immaculate Mrs. Bashaw in the same room with a frail sister! *Sister*, indeed! Away with you, you wicked hussy! But Mrs. Bashaw is a Christian lady. So she advised the girl to repent, but of course she could not take her into her house. Go forth, you wicked one! God may forgive you, and so does Mrs. Bashaw with her tongue; but so far as she is concerned she will not give you a chance of leading a virtuous life, to save your body from prostitution and your soul from eternal damnation. She is too respectable for that. "Go," said Mrs. Bashaw, "sin no more, and send the Superintendent to me." The Superintendent was sorry that the girl did not suit her customer, but the right article had just come in. The cunning Superintendent always tries to get rid of her worst goods first, but Mrs. Bashaw is just as cunning, and will not be so imposed upon.

Enter the right article. The girl is tall, healthy-looking, neatly dressed, and respectful in her manners. She informs Mrs. Bashaw, that her name is Susan Vagg, and that she is three-and-twenty.

Susan Vagg, you are laying it on there. You are only twenty unless you came into the world three years old, or unless, like one of my Hibernian friends, you were born when your mother was out, and she did not know of the event for three years afterwards. That little fib will add two pounds to your wages; but still Susan it is a fib, and it is quite as naughty for the eldest Miss Vagg to say she is older than she is, as it is for the eldest Miss Bashaw to be five years travelling from seventeen to nineteen.

Mrs. Bashaw having asked Susan if she was honest, and if she could get a good character from her last place, proceeded to explain the sort of service she wanted her to render. She must rise at half-past five without being called. The house must be kept beautifully clean, for Mrs. Bashaw cannot abide dirty corners. The heavy things are put out, but the light articles of apparel will have to be washed by Susan. The cooking, though plain, must be perfect of its kind. After the dinner things are cleared away, the kitchen must be made tidy, and Susan must be dressed ready for waiting. When the nurse is out or assisting the elder young ladies with their toilet, Susan must take care of the children. Susan must go to church on Sunday morning with the family—not of course to sit in the family pew, but with the boy in the free seats. Susan is to have one holiday a month, but she cannot go out until twelve, and must be home by nine. No followers are permitted. Gossiping at the door is strictly prohibited. Half a pint of beer *per diem* is allowed to each servant. Wages £11 per annum.

Susan courtsies, and accepts the conditions. Call this hiring or buying, which you like: it is, at all events, obtaining human flesh and blood at a cheap rate. You say that Susan is not bound to serve Mrs. Bashaw. Would she do so if she could help it? Would you, my fair friend, accept such service? Let us have a glance at Susan in her new home, and I am sure you will shudder at the bare idea of such a fate.

One day in the service of Mrs. Bashaw is so like unto another that one day's story is the story of her servant's life. The alarum goes off at half-past five—Mrs. Bashaw kindly provides an alarum for the servant's bedroom—and Susan gets up, lights her candle, puts on her clothes, and steals down stairs. At her entrance into the kitchen the beetles, with the exception of those which are trodden under her feet, run to their holes. The fire is lighted as quickly as it can be with the small quantity of wood that Mrs. Bashaw gives out for that purpose. The coal-cellar door being open, the cat comes out, and purring, rubs herself against the servant. Well, Susan, we don't like cats, but we quite understand that even feline sympathy is better than no sympathy at all. By the time the kitchen fire is lighted the boy puts in an appearance, and in the wash-house sets to work to clean the knives and forks. Susan next *does* the dining-room, and woe unto her if the carpet is not well swept and the furniture well dusted! At seven o'clock the milkwoman comes, and here veracity compels us to tell of one of Susan's peccadilloes. She takes a good drink out of the pint-and-a-half of milk, and fills up the jug with water. Surely the recording angel will blot out the record of this offence with a tear of mercy. Mrs. Bashaw is such an excellent wife, such a careful housekeeper, that she permits no waste of food in her establishment. After evening prayers she descends to the basement and locks up the pantry, so that the servants may not be tempted by the pangs of hunger to eat a breakfast before the regular hour. Now rising at half-past five, especially in the winter, engenders a very voracious appetite long before seven, and Susan is not strong-minded enough to resist its cravings until after the family breakfast at eight. Therefore, being deprived of bread, she purloins the milk. After the refreshing draught, Susan hearthstones her steps. A nasty job at any time, but particularly nasty when the rising sun is obscured by fog, or when the morning is cold. Soon after seven Susan takes up hot water to the nursery, and lights the nursery fire. Then she sets light to the fire in the young ladies' dressing-room, for it is not healthy for the dear girls to dress in a cold room. Then rings the bell of the mistress's room, and to that apartment Susan has likewise to convey hot water—for Mrs. Bashaw is delicate, and cannot bear the shock of cold water. By eight o'clock breakfast must be on the table, the bacon being properly cooked, and the abundant supply of toast, nicely browned. Mrs. Bashaw herself makes the tea, as such a superlative housekeeper will never trust the key of her caddy in the hands of a domestic creature.

At half-past eight the boy rings a hand-bell in the hall, which is the signal for morning prayers. The servants march into the dining-room, each one carrying a cane-bottomed chair, for it would not do to let the domestic creatures sit on the chairs which are used by the family. The servants are ranged at one end of the room, near to the door, and quite at the other end of the room is the family group. What condescension! What a beautiful illustration of Christian humility! Surely it would be unreasonable to complain that the servants are not greeted with a "Good Morning." Enough that they are allowed to sit in the same room with their superiors, whilst the Bible is read, whilst Mr. Bashaw prays, and whilst Mrs. Bashaw, covering her face with a square of the finest linen, may be supposed by those who cannot read the human heart, to be joining in the supplications which proceed from the lips of her husband. Fortunate domestic creatures thus to have the Gospel offered to them—at the end of a long pair of tongs!

The beds being made, and the bed-rooms being put in order, Susan has the honour of receiving her mistress in the kitchen. Mrs. Bashaw inspects the dust-hole, to see if the cinders have been properly sifted, and that nothing has been thrown away that might have been burnt. Then the lady looks into the grease-pot. Mrs. Bashaw allows no perquisites, but sells her own grease. After giving instructions for the dinner, Mrs. Bashaw performs her daily task of fault-finding. Some corner of the house is not so clean as it might be, or Mrs. Bashaw suspects that Susan ate some of the tart after it left the table, or that Susan has been gossiping with some of the tradesmen, or that Susan wastes her mistress's time by letter-writing or with fancy work, or that Susan has had the impertinence to mildly rebuke the insolence of one of the children. If Susan remained twenty-years in the service of Mrs. Bashaw, she would not hear one word of commendation. She may work from morning till night, and from week's end to week's end, she may endure with imperturbable good humour the irritability of the master, the haughty snubbing of the young ladies, and the nagging of her mistress; she may try with all her heart and soul to be kind, respectful, and assiduous, yet, in the eyes of such an immaculate housekeeper as Mrs. Bashaw, she will always be an unprofitable servant.

The family dines at three. If there is any cold meat, that, with suet pudding, is the fare of the denizens of the kitchen. If by accident they are compelled to dine off the hot joint, the part they are to cut at, which we may be sure is not the best part, is designated by the mistress. When the family dinner is over, and the kitchen tidied, Susan enjoys the inestimable privilege of going to her bedroom, making her bed and dressing herself. At six o'clock there is master's dinner, and at seven o'clock the family tea. At half-past eight the hot water is taken to the dining-room, in order that the master and mistress may imbibe a little stimulant. Except answering the bell, and doing her share of kitchen needlework, Susan is now at liberty. At liberty to sit down in the under-ground kitchen, but not at liberty to see a friend and to enjoy a few minutes' social intercourse. She can employ her leisure in mending her clothes, or in reading tracts provided for her edification by her most

Christian mistress. At ten o'clock, whether there be company or not, the hand-bell is again rung, and the servants, carrying their cane chairs in their hands, go into the dining-room for evening prayers. After prayers they say, according to instructions, "Good night, sir!" "Good night, ma'am!" Susan goes to bed, and her light must be out in ten minutes. It is wasteful to keep it burning longer, and Mrs. Bashaw allows no other waste in her house besides the waste of the flesh and blood of her domestic creatures.

Such is an ordinary day's work in the service of Mrs. Bashaw. When there is company, or when there is sickness in the house, or when the washing is about, the work is much harder. All this for eleven pounds a year! Work, work, from morning till night, and no rest; the best years of life passed in drudgery, and with no more personal freedom than is accorded to a felon. I grant that the flesh of oxen and sheep is dear ; but, my fair friend, you cannot deny that human flesh and blood, white, Caucasian flesh and blood, is dirt cheap in this great city of London.

What becomes of Susan Vagg ? If she is very, exceptionally fortunate, she gets married. Her opportunities for marrying are few. She is only permitted to see the tradesmen, and they are not the marrying sort. The butcher is a fast lad—a Don Juan in blue. The Grocer's man is a cut above the servant, and the cat's-meat man is a cut below. The baker's man is the right sort, but what is one amongst so many? The policeman is only a cupboard lover. As for the postman, I think no one ever knew that functionary to be guilty of flirtation. It is an odd coincidence; but I am persuaded that a smart-looking man never yet was employed by the post-office. Susan gets followers, it is true; but she can see so little of them that the young man she "walks with" seldom walks to church with her.

Perhaps Susan gets sick and then she is sent to the hospital. Mrs. Bashaw will not allow a sick domestic creature to remain in her well-conducted house. Perhaps Susan gives notice to quit, and gets into easier service, and she certainly cannot get into any harder service. What becomes of the majority of such domestic creatures as Susan Vagg must be told with bated breath, and in a manner not to offend ears polite.

There are in London 50,000 women who exist by prostitution. To their career must be charged a large part of the vice, the misery, and the crime that afflict society. Of these 50,000 women not less than half have been at one time or other domestic servants. Are you grieving to-day, Mrs. Bashaw, that your son has sacrificed every prospect in life for the sake of a horrid creature—a certain wicked woman named Rose Cavendish? Madam, that Rose Cavendish was a domestic creature once, such as Susan Vagg. Be careful how you curse her. Let me tell you, madam, that if you had been tempted as she was tempted, you, too, would have fallen. What can be expected when a young woman is cut off from all human sympathy and kindness, and then hears the simulated professions of human affection? It is as certain that she will fall as it is that she will die if she swallows poison. We do not in the least excuse prostitution, but it is not to be denied that it is to a great extent brought about by the way in which our domestic servants are treated.

One word to you, and such as you, Mrs. Bashaw. We are not deceived, nor are you deceived by your family praying and hysterical maunderings about faith in Christianity. We take it that no one can believe in the Gospel of mercy and love, and yet treat a human creature as you treat your servants. In your heart, if you have a heart, you look upon religion as a mere sham, and you only bow at the name of Him who came to earth in great humility because it is fashionable to do so. But, Mrs. Bashaw, if there is anything in it—if there be such things as judgment and retribution! We once heard an old woman counsel her daughter to wash her feet and put on clean linen before she went on a journey. If an accident happened it would be awkward and disgaceful when the clean outside garments were lifted to find dirtiness beneath. Mrs. Bashaw, would it not be well to try to cleanse your heart a little before you go on a certain long journey, for fear of accidents, for fear there are such things as judgment and retribution for the deeds done on earth? As a beginning, try to treat your domestic servants at least as well as your husband treats his horse, and as you treat your lap dog.

Mrs. Bashaw is the type of a class; yet, thank God, not the type of the vast majority of English matrons; but those who are much better than Mrs. Bashaw often treat their servants nearly as badly. What the human heart yearns for is sympathy, and this they will not give to their domestics. We do not plead for that familiarity that breeds contempt, but for that kindly familiarity that breeds good-will and happiness. What harm would result from shaking hands with the servants after the nightly prayers? What harm would result from the children, when they come home from visiting or from school, shaking hands with the servants? Why not talk to the domestic servants about the affairs of the heart? They need guidance, and who is so fit to guide them as the matron of the house? Change our present system, and we shall no more be bored with constant complaints about bad servants. Change our system, and thousands of women, now unhappy and an easy prey to temptation, will be happy and virtuous. A little kindness will gladden our homes and mitigate the immorality that now disgraces our city. This is a reform that is not only demanded by duty, but also by interest. In a hundred different ways the evil that we do unto the least of our brethren and sisters is visited upon us. Let the poor rot in fever dens, and the winds of Heaven will carry the pestilence to our rich homes. If we by neglect or unkindness expose our domestic servants to sore temptations, we suffer as well as they do. We always reap as we sow, though we do not always perceive the connection between the sowing and the reaping.

We almost wish we had not written on this subject. We

wish some one who better knows how to plead the cause of humanity had undertaken it. Oh, that our feeble voice could be heard by the matrons of England! Oh, that our countrywomen would consider! Then, indeed, there would be a change of system, the great multitude of domestic servants would be happy, and our sons might walk in the streets without at every corner being solicited by fallen women. Remember, ye wives and mothers, that in London alone there are 50,000 fallen women, and of that number at least one-half were at one time in their lives domestic servants. We will no more bemoan the feebleness of our utterances and the coldness of our pleading. If that fact will not move you, then neither would you be persuaded though we spake with the tongue of an angel.

OUR SUBURBAN HOTEL.

---o---

No more pen and ink for to-day. We ought "to make copy," but we cannot. Confound it, that can't be right. What we *cannot* do we *ought not* to do. In fact as Professor O'Keefe taught us in our youth, it would be a positive wrong to do that which we cannot do, and fortunately it is impossible. So, you little fiend, go back to your sender, and tell him that the copy promised to-day will be ready tomorrow. It is no use raving, thou cruel and voracious printer. You say we ought to keep our promise. We do not agree with you. We contend that we ought not, because we cannot. We are neither sick nor tired, but we cannot work. We have darkened the room, but the sunbeams enter through tiny crevices and invite us to go forth. We smoke a pipe, but for all that heart and brain are for the nonce miles away from our work. We drink tea, which merely increases the irritation. We cannot write. Oh, what a comfort that we resolve not to do so! In an instant the feeling of weariness is gone, and instead of being in a state of savageness we are now all benevolence. That organ which we have been so remorselessly condemning is, after all, not without its uses. It amuses children, and really the tunes are very well set. We pull up the blind, open the window, and throw a penny to the grinder. We shall be twice mulcted for that charity in days to come.

We soon get up a party for an excursion. Our friends happen to know that our little retreat in the country is one of the jolliest places that can be found, and that guests are there entertained with the best of viands and wines. So when we dropped in upon one or two good fellows and invited them to dine with us at—let us call it "The Mitre," the assent was ready and hearty.

We grant that the hotels of France and America are gigantic and splendid. We do not deny that the modern hotels of London are excellent and superb. We appreciate the luxury and *cuisine* of the *Grosvenor*. We are duly impressed with the grandeur of the *Langham*, the *Charing Cross*, the *Palace*, and establishments of that class. Yet these are more or less imitations, or perhaps we should say that they are cosmopolitan. But we have in England some establishments that are essentially English. We do not now refer to country hotels, but to those minor hotels that are to be found in the suburbs. When American gentlemen first come to this country they deride our native oysters, and dilate upon the superiority and lusciousness of the American bivalves. After a little while our cousins change their opinions, and become fond of our sweet, delicate little natives, and confess that, although the American people beat all creation, including the solar system and the entire universe, yet that in the matter of oysters the old country—which they love and abuse—is a little ahead. In like manner we are convinced that, although an American would at first treat with supreme contempt our metropolitan suburban hotels, yet upon a closer acquaintance he would be persuaded that, like our oysters, they are unequalled. The fact is, they combine the comforts of the English home with the comforts of an hotel.

The "Mitre" is an old-fashioned house, built when George the First was King of England, and of that empire upon which the sun never sets, "because," said a cute Yankee "Providence knows what British wickedness is, and will not trust it in the dark." The "Mitre" suggests fossilation. It seems as if it had left off growing old about thirty years ago, and had remained unaffected by the flight of time. The furniture is not modern, but in most excellent condition.

The rooms are not gaudy or glaring, or redolent of the prevailing cheap free trade decorations, yet all things look fresh and pleasant. The whole place, we repeat, suggests that it had left off growing old about thirty years ago. It looks as if in the year 1835 the house had been put to rights and had remained in perfect order ever since. The walls of the sitting-rooms are furnished with some quaint old prints. In our room is an engraving of an actor who was in the zenith of his fame when our grandmothers were singing love ditties to the accompaniment of the harpsicord. On either side of the defunct actor are animal engravings of an ante-Landseer period. We learn from the printed inscriptions that the one represents bulls fighting, and the other horses fighting. The information is useful, for without it we might have been slightly in doubt as to the species of the animals, and we should not have known whether they were fighting or playing. We daresay our grandsires were impressed with the beauty of these engravings, and we confess to liking them. We hope our room will never be deprived of these quaint mural embellishments.

Our room is not the best in the house, although it suits us best. It is quiet and cozy. It has no look-out, but that we do not care for. The waiter often solicits us to use a front room, but his solicitations are in vain. The waiter has a weakness for the said front room. We call it the Cenci room. Everybody, from young ladies with a taste for painting, to artists who paint at so much per foot, seem to esteem it a prescriptive right to grossly caricature the Cenci. Look at the " Mitre " copy. The golden hue of the hair is translated into the colour of egg. The face, much in the wooden Dutch doll style, wears the expression of the face of a young lady who has been eating too freely of toffee, and is suffering from a species of bastard sea-sickness. But the throat is the most provoking distortion. The Cenci throat is an exquisite creation; but the " Mitre " copy, like most other copies, merely gives us a throat that indicates mumps, swollen tonsils, stiff neck, and embryo carbuncles. However, the waiter tells us the picture is greatly admired by the Germans, who on Sundays during the summer frequent the " Mitre." The Teutonic Sunday swell is evidently not an authority in matters of art, though he knows all about bitter beer and showy dressing.

We enter the " Mitre." Genial smile from the landlord, ditto from the landlady, ditto from the daughters of the " Mitre." We ascend the stairs. Chambermaid drops a curtsey, and tries to look as if she did not know that our visit was, at least, half-a-crown in her pocket. Waiter bows gracefully, and, after inquiry as to our sanitary condition, marshals us into our room. As we have one or two friends with us, would we prefer the front room? No, we would not; but we retired for a brief while with the waiter to the said front room.

The waiter looks solemn. We are about to order dinner. We have the too common human weakness of supposing that we can arrange a dinner rather better than anybody else; and the waiter dumbly flatters our vanity by looking as if he was about to hear a momentous revelation. We take the bill of fare in one hand, and with the other we diplomatically twirl our moustache. Are there any oysters to be had? Certainly, sir. Then let the first course consist of a plate of three oysters for each guest, the bivalves lying in their upper shells. With the oysters to be served lemon, cayenne pepper, and thin slices of brown bread, slightly buttered. It is a vulgar error to put the butter on too thickly. Any wine with the oysters? Yes, just one glass of *Vin de gras*, which, of course, must be served in large green glasses. The soup must be thin, but withal slightly, very slightly *piquante*, and as the soup is light we will take brown sherry with it. How many sorts of fish will we take? Two, at most. Let there be salmon cutlets for those who choose to play havoc with the appetite at an early stage of the dinner, and let there be fillet of sole fried. The *chef* at the " Mitre " excels in fried fillet of sole. Up they come, brown all over, so dry as not to soil the snowy napkin on which they are placed, and crisp without being hard. With the salmon let there be cucumber, not cut too thin, so as to be knify, and dressed with oil, white vinegar, and white pepper. We do not allow any potatoes with the fish, out of consideration for the digestive organs of our guests. As to *entrées*, we leave them to the *chef*, with the special injunction that they are not to include any admixture of ham, and that there must not be any flavouring of angelica root. Now for the *piece de resistance*. The waiter respectfully intimates that there is a Dartmoor leg of mutton—" Such a little beauty, sir "—that has been hanging in the larder for a week. Capital! Let that be well roasted by a quick fire, and for gravy we will not resort to the stock-tub, but be content with that which flows from the joint when it is cut— cut longways, and not in the barbarous family fashion. With the mutton a few potatoes fried, not boiled. With the roast let us have still hock, cold as ice can make it. Then let us have a vegetable course of asparagus and artichokes. We abhor the system of spoiling the flavour of delicate vegetables by eating them with meat. A plover's egg after the vegetables would be agreeable. Wild duck, or anything that is birdy and gamey, will complete the courses. "Any sweets?" No, we do not wish our friends to remember our hospitality by a headache. Any maccaroni cheese? Certainly not: we do not wish to spoil our good dinner by such a ponderous addition. To concede a little to the prejudices of our friends, we will permit the introduction of cheese— but not Stilton. Let it be Gruyere or Parmesan. Dessert we eschew. With the port, sherry and claret, let there be an abundant supply of unsweetened biscuits. The conference is over, and at the appointed hour the dinner is served without any mistake, and we and the *chef* of the "Mitre" win golden opinions from our guests.

Some irate housewife remarks that it is of course easy to get a good dinner if one is reckless of expense. We beg to state that, a first-rate dinner at our suburban hotel costs us far less than a second-rate dinner at home. Besides, unlike

John Gilpin's wife, we are not particularly frugal-minded when intent on pleasure.

As soon as we are through our wine our excellent landlord enters. He hopes the wine has been to our liking? The response is a chorus of commendation. He favours us with a concise history of his stock of wines, and very solemnly protests against cheap stuff—remarkable sherry at one and sevenpence, and celebrated old port at one and ninepence per bottle. On one occasion he met a friend in town who invited him to take a glass of wine. In they walked to a kind of stores, and glasses of sherry were placed before them. Our host drank his off and was nearly poisoned. "Why gentlemen, it was sour ditchwater. No wonder my friend threw down a shilling to pay for the two glasses and got sixpence change. I was never so badly treated in my life." After this story he politely invited us to visit his cellar—mine host is not free from "vaulting ambition"—to crack a bottle of his '34. The cordial invitation is cordially accepted, and without more ado, we descend. *Facilis descensus Averni*, but it is not particularly easy to descend to the "Mitre Cellars," and if you are not careful, head or hat will be bruised. Now the "Mitre" cellars would be a source of pride to any gentleman in the land. They are not large, but compact, and of a pleasant equable temperature. The wines are labelled as to sorts and dates, and some of them have been reposing for forty years. Having seen and tasted the wine curiosities we glance at the spiders, which are the most gigantic we have ever seen. They appear to be in good relations with their master, and come out of their nest webs at his bidding. Then from the '34 bin a bottle is carefully lifted, carefully placed on a wooden cradle, the cork carefully drawn and handed round for inspection; the wine is decanted, without a spot of beeswing or crust dimming its ruby brightness, and finally we drink it. Oh, what nectar! Oh, what nectar to cure the cholic, and all the ills that the stomach is heir to! Oh, what nectar to make glad the heart of man! It needed heroic resolution to tear ourselves away and to refuse a second bottle.

A cup of tea for the merry and wise, grog for those who like it, and cigars for all. Time is up, and so, shaking hands with our host, and with a gracious bow from our waiter, we depart. We have not seen much of the country, yet, as we are borne to town in a comfortable carriage, converted for the occasion into a smoking saloon, we agree that we have had a jolly day, and that for some inscrutable reason a dinner in town is never so enjoyable as a dinner at a suburban hotel. We hope the "Mitre" and places of its kind will not fall victims to the joint-stock mania. In town an hotel manager is desirable, but our little place in the suburbs would not be *our* little place if it were not under the charge of our excellent friend, the considerate and humorous host.

www.ingramcontent.com/pod-product-compliance
Lightning Source LLC
Chambersburg PA
CBHW020058170426
43199CB00009B/330